BIPOLAR DISORDER

The New Gratitude Journal for an Awesome Life

(Living with Bipolar daily and how to progress through Bipolar)

Brenda Carmichael

Published by Oliver Leish

Brenda Carmichael

All Rights Reserved

Bipolar Disorder: The New Gratitude Journal for an
Awesome Life (Living with Bipolar daily and how to progress
through Bipolar)

ISBN 978-1-77485-092-3

Legal & Disclaimer

The information contained in this book is not designed to replace or take the place of any form of medicine or professional medical advice. The information in this book has been provided for educational and entertainment purposes only.

The information contained in this book has been compiled from sources deemed reliable, and it is accurate to the best of the Author's knowledge; however, the Author cannot guarantee its accuracy and validity and cannot be held liable for any errors or omissions. Changes are periodically made to this book. You must consult your doctor or get professional medical advice before using any of the suggested remedies, techniques, or information in this book.

Upon using the information contained in this book, you agree to hold harmless the Author from and against any damages, costs, and expenses, including any legal fees potentially resulting from the application of any of the information provided by this guide. This disclaimer applies to any damages or injury caused by the use and application, whether directly or indirectly, of any advice or information presented, whether for breach of contract, tort, negligence, personal injury, criminal intent, or under any other cause of action.

You agree to accept all risks of using the information presented inside this book. You need to consult a professional medical practitioner in order to ensure you are both able and healthy enough to participate in this program.

Table of Contents

Chapter 1: Defining Bipolar Disorder

Have you ever been around a person who has frequent mood swings, or do you experience mood swings yourself? Are there times that you feel delirious with happiness, and then suddenly something happens and you plunge to an emotional low? While it's normal to experience mood swings from time to time, frequent and unmanageable mood swings can be an indicator of something more serious: bipolar disorder.

According to psychiatric experts, about 4 percent of Americans and 2 percent of the entire global population actually experience this condition. However, only some cases actually get diagnosed because the symptoms of this condition are not as pronounced as those of other psychological disorders. Many people don't think of mood swings as an indicator of something serious. Often, we just think that someone's "having a bad day" or that they "woke up on the wrong side of the bed."

Are you or someone you know experiencing mood swings often? Here's how to tell if those are just regular ones or if they're probably caused by something far more serious.

Bipolar Disorder: What is it?

Bipolar disorder is a psychiatric disorder often associated with disruptive and extreme mood swings alongside fluctuating energy levels as well. These episodes of elation and depression are very different from the normal peak of emotions that regular people experience in their daily lives.

The term bipolar is actually derived from these people's tendency to shift from one extreme mood polarity to the other almost instantly during manic-depressive episodes. Other terms for this condition are manic depression and manic depressive disorder, and it is often related to consecutive episodes of hypomania and depression.

Bipolar Mood Swings

On normal days, people with bipolar disorder are pretty much the same as regular people in terms of moods and emotions. However, when something triggers a manic depressive attack, their emotional and mood levels either spike up or plunge down, almost successively.

These mood swings could be a case of mild hypomania (elation) or a mild case of "the blues," but extreme cases often cause

3

incapacitation. A person ceases to function normally and loses interest in everyday activities that he used to enjoy, becoming highly unstable and even suicidal at times.

Extreme episodes might also coincide with psychosis and hallucination episodes wherein the patient cannot distinguish reality from fantasy. The frequency of manic-depressive episodes could be far-in-between or very frequent depending on certain factors such as causality and triggers.

Bipolar Symptoms

There are two main sets of symptoms associated with bipolar disorder, depending on whether the patient is having manic/hypomanic or depressive mood episodes. A separate chapter will elaborate on these two conditions separately, but for now, let us return our focus on the common signs and symptoms that may indicate that a person is having a manic-depressive attack.

Mania symptoms

Mania or hypomania refers to an extremely high mood and emotional levels, often characterized by feelings of euphoria or elation. During a manic episode, a bipolar person feels very confident and invincible; his self-esteem also becomes bloated to the point that he thinks he can do anything. This, in turn, can alter his subjective judgment and his ability to make sound decisions.

If you're around a bipolar person during a manic episode, you'd notice that he begins to talk at a much quicker pace than what is normal for him, as if he has no control over his words and just blurts out everything that comes to his mind. His thought processes go haywire, so the things he talks about might be flitting and disorganized. He might feel a sudden urge to do a lot of things at once even if it doesn't seem possible at the time. He might come up with strange solutions for a totally different problem, and he will insist on doing things his way—aggressively.

During manic episodes, bipolar individuals are more prone to doing something risque and often dangerous—things that they won't do during their normal mood phases. For instance, they might become more promiscuous or easily influenced to use harmful substances like alcohol and illegal drugs. They might gamble their money away or use it to buy things they don't really want or need.

Bipolar patients also aren't able to concentrate and are easily distractible during these episodes. They might become unreliable and decide to skip work or school entirely because of the euphoria they experience. At worst, a patient will experience delusions and hallucinations and believe that these are real.

Depression symptoms

In contrast to mania, depressive episodes are instances when a bipolar patient's mood level drops completely, like entering a black hole wherein he cannot find interest in anything beyond his emotions. During these episodes, a person might feel a bleak feeling of despair or hopelessness as if he believes that he is doomed.

Extreme and uncharacteristic sadness for no apparent reason, sometimes to the point of thinking suicidal thoughts and acting on them, is also one common symptom of a depressive episode. People who are depressed also often have difficulty sleeping coupled with symptoms of anxiety disorders and feelings of guilt. At this point, the patient is convinced that he is at fault for everything that has gone wrong in his life, a project, or anything that he is involved with.

Depressive episodes are also accompanied by changes in a person's eating and sleeping patterns. Either a person will engage in binge eating and gain weight, or stop eating altogether, losing weight in the process. Depressed bipolars also often feel easily tired and restless, and they stop enjoying the things that they normally loved doing.

During these episodes, you might find it very hard to get the attention of a bipolar patient. He can't focus; he's quick to become angry, annoyed or irritated at the most trivial things. The worst episodes can render a bipolar individual to withdraw from routine activity and social mingling; they end up not attending school or work because of their depressive mood.

Mixed episodes

For bipolar people, symptoms of mania and depression might manifest in a single instance. These episodes are often called mixed episodes because the patient experiences mood and emotional highs and lows at the same time. Thus, the symptoms above are not exclusive to each other, and in some cases, you might notice symptoms from both types of bipolar episodes.

Causes of Bipolar Disorder

Bipolar disorder is a complex condition that could not be blamed on any singular factor. A confluence of several causes might increase a person's risk to develop this disorder once he reaches a certain age. Here are some of the most common causes agreed upon by experts.

Genetic causes

There is some evidence that bipolar disorder tends to be passed on genetically within families. For instance, parents who have developed or experienced bipolar disorder at least once in their lives are more likely than "normal" parents to have bipolar children.

This does not mean, however, that people who have relatives with bipolar disorder automatically develop the disease. Their risk of contracting the condition is higher in them than in people who don't have any bipolar family members.

Neurological makeup

Another possible factor that can increase a person's risk to develop bipolar disorder is the way his brain is structured. Many psychiatrists and physiologists agree that bipolar disorder can be considered a neural disorder, which means it has something to do with the functions and processes of a person's brain and central nervous system.

Modern technological advancements in the field of medical diagnosis such as functional magnetic resonance imaging (fMRI) make it possible to capture images of the brain while it is at work. Several studies involving brain imaging of bipolar patients showed that their brain structures and processes are different from those of "regular" people.

One study even discovered that brain development in bipolar children follows a pattern that is very similar to that of another psychiatric disorder—schizophrenia. These abnormal brain patterns are commonly linked to the dramatic changes in the mood of bipolar patients.

Hormonal imbalance

Certain hormonal substances in the brain and other parts of the nervous system are also possibly responsible for the development of bipolar disorder. Hormones play an important role in the neurotransmitters and brain processes, and if something goes wrong with them, it might also result in a manic or depressive episode.

Environmental causes

A person with biological and genetic risks doesn't necessarily develop bipolar disorder over time, unless he is exposed to psycho-social conditions that can trigger an episode. There is strong evidence that links a person's familial upbringing, social status, and relationships to his tendency to become bipolar.

Recent traumatic occurrences, disturbances, and conflict in interpersonal relationships are all possible factors which may cause a person to experience depressive or manic episodes at first. Repetition and the frequency of an individual's exposure to these factors may determine whether his singular episodes will lead to a chronic bipolar disorder. For instance, a stressful childhood and having abusive parents are both factors which might cause an earlier onset of bipolar disorder.

Triggers

Once a person has developed bipolar disorders, it becomes wired to his system until medical or therapeutical intervention comes into play. Bipolar people are generally normal most of the time, until something triggers an episode of mania or depression. Triggers are external factors which usually render a bipolar individual's thought processes and behavioural patterns abnormal for a certain period.

Bipolar people find it more difficult to handle certain situations, a hindrance which makes them unable to lead normal lives. Here are just some of the things they couldn't cope with that a regular person can usually handle well.

Stress. Stressful events and activities, such as the death of a loved one or overwork, are among the most common triggers of manic-depressive episodes. Sudden and drastic changes (both positive and negative) may also cause undue stress upon a bipolar individual as these are things that he might not be able to handle.

Substance use. Bipolars and addictive substances don't mix. While substance use and abuse are not direct causes of bipolar disorder, they have been known to magnify the effects of mania and depression. Depending on the substance, a bipolar patient can experience manic episodes (Hallucinatory drugs like cocaine and LSD are potential manic triggers.) or depressive ones (due to alcohol, morphine, and other tranquilizers).

Medication. Certain drugs have been known to trigger manic episodes. This is especially true for psychotic and anti-depressant drugs as well as cough syrups and medication for colds.

Seasonal changes. Some bipolars can experience manic and depressive episodes depending on the current season. Mania is more often experienced during summer while depression often sets in during fall or winter.

Lack of sleep. Sleep-deprived bipolars often experience mania because their senses go into overdrive due to the continuous functioning of their brain without enough rest. This is why they need to establish regular sleep routines and schedules.

Food intake. Certain foods, especially sugary and starchy ones as well as chocolates, have been known to trigger manic episodes in bipolar individuals. These substances are known to cause a spike in blood sugar levels and cause hormonal imbalance in neurotransmitters. After experiencing sugar-induced mania, the patient will soon fall into an extremely low mood with a depleted energy level.

Chapter 2: Signs And Symptoms Of Bipolar Disorder

Mental health practitioners have a guideline in diagnosing whether an individual has a mental disorder or not. Following DSM-5, these are the signs and symptoms to look out for people who are suspected to have bipolar disorder. The list includes symptoms to look out for specific form of bipolar disorder.

DSM-5 divided the spectrum of bipolar disorder intro three forms. The three forms retained the similarity with regards on experiencing duality of mood. However, the three forms of bipolar disorder are differentiated according to their severity and possible occurrence. This means that there might be significant behavioral difference among the three forms of bipolar disorder.

Bipolar I Disorder

This disorder is formerly known as manic-depressive disorder. As the name implies, this disorder entails the person to experience single full-blown mania (intense elation) during an individual's lifetime and a series of bipolar episodes. Bipolar episode means a sudden shift of mood from elation to depression and/or vice versa.

A person who has this disorder will likely to display at least once in the individual's life characteristic of a full-blown mania which includes erratic behaviors such as engagement to substance use, casual sex, extreme sports (when in fact the person does not usually engage in it), mindless spending, and other behaviors that can be considered as risky and the person is not likely to engage in prior to the onset. The person may even be required to be hospitalized in order to control his or her extreme behavior. Full-blown mania may last for a day or a week.

Another sign to look out for is the bipolar episode that the person displays, which may happen before or after the occurrence of the full-blown mania. The person could appear jovial and enthusiastic at one time then suddenly becomes irritable and delve into depression. This cycle tends to happen over and over again, and may be seen as part of the person's personality where in fact, it is actually part of the individual's mental problem.

Bipolar II Disorder

Bipolar II is a milder form of bipolar disorder. Diagnosis of this specific disorder includes experience of at least one major depressive episode and at least one episode of hypomania (a milder form of mania).

Hypomania is similar to full-blown mania, only that the hypomania is less severe. People with hypomania may display delusions of extravagance by setting up goals that appear unrealistic to the observer. Person can be seen as active, and may even lack sleep because of efforts to finish the set 'goals'. People with hypomania tend to be creative and actually showcase productivity during these episodes. However, their risky behavior puts them into a difficult position as like the manic person, they might just plunge into the behavior without really thinking of the consequences of their actions. Unlike full-blown mania which may occur once or twice, hypomania persistently occurs and can be seen regularly in an individual.

In addition, people with bipolar II disorder also experiences major depression. They often exhibit characteristics of a depressed person such as lack of interest in any activities and inability to feel pleasure in anything they do. Most of the times, people with bipolar II disorder only see the aspect of depression and even professionals make a mistake of diagnosing the disorder as major depressive disorder. Occurrence of hypomania is more often than not seen as 'normal' and is therefore overlooked when professionals do diagnosis.

Cyclothymic Disorder

Symptoms for this disorder should be present for at least 2 years in adults and 1 year for children and adolescents. Symptoms include recurring episodes of mild depression and mild mania. People with this disorder exhibit similar symptoms to bipolar II disorder. However, these symptoms are less severe in form. This is mainly manifested through shifts between being in high spirits and being irritated. Though they may exhibit less risky behaviors, they are more likely to malfunction in their interpersonal relationships because others will not understand their sudden shifts of mood. It is also likely that they will not understand themselves and will therefore bring more problems to their plate.

Note: There is no absolute measure in diagnosing bipolar disorder, which is also true for all other mental disorders. The symptoms listed by DSM-5 will be very helpful in evaluating whether you or someone you know could have a bipolar disorder. Caution should be exercised in labeling someone though, and to ensure precision in labeling, refer the person suspected of having bipolar disorder to a certified professional for accurate diagnosis.

Chapter 3: Available Treatments

Treatment is necessary and crucial. While the primary and conventional treatment remains to be medical under the supervision of physicians specializing in mental or psychiatric disorders, there are other treatments that are equally effective. You may benefit the most from a combination of these treatments.

Steps to Benefit from the Best Treatment

To start benefiting from the best treatment for bipolar, here are simple steps you can follow:

Consult your physician or a brain specialist to get a professional diagnosis of your condition.

The ability to recognize the symptoms is a big help, and getting a confirmation from an expert will lead you to the best treatment. Professional diagnosis will also be able to either rule out or identify other health conditions.

Through the diagnosis, you will be able to determine the type of bipolar that you have. Discuss with your health expert the prognosis of your condition and all possible options to treat and manage your condition.

You must be aware that while there is no cure for the disorder, you can still live a full life with minimal interruptions from the disorder.

If the symptoms of your bipolar condition is mild to moderate, or if it is hypomania or mild depression that you are experiencing, you are better off with natural treatment for bipolar.

Even with moderate to severe symptoms, you should try to lessen your dependence on drug-based medication as much as possible, and choose to treat your condition with natural methods.

Strengthen your support system. This is crucial in dealing with the symptoms of your condition. When your support system is solid and strong, it will be easier for you to manage and control the symptoms of bipolar disorder.

Your support system may consist of the following: your family and relatives, friends, bipolar support community or group, and health experts such as your physician and therapist.

Medical Treatment

Medical treatment includes consultations with your physician, counselor or therapist, and the taking of prescriptive medicines for your mania and depression. The drug-based medicines are meant for mood stabilization. Your physician may also prescribe maintenance medication which you will take on a long-term basis, or probably for a lifetime.

Here are the types of drug-based medicines for bipolar: anti-mania medicines, anti-depression medicines, anti-psychotic medicines, maintenance and prevention medication, anti-anxiety medicines, and sedatives.

Part of your medical treatment will be therapeutic sessions with a professional counselor or therapist. During the sessions, your therapist will encourage you to talk freely and discuss how you feel, what is bothering you, what you are thinking, and similar stuff that will help lighten and restore your normal mood.

Therapy may also include the following: ECT or electroconvulsive therapy, light therapy, DBS or deep brain stimulation, and RTMS or repetitive transcranial magnetic stimulation. These therapies target the brain to treat the condition from inside out.

Natural Remedies

Several natural remedies are available and are worth focusing on in treating your condition. If you can manage and control the symptoms using only natural methods, you will be able to free yourself from the risk of side effects that normally happens with drug-based medications.

If you have not yet started your drug-based medication, consider natural remedies as your primary treatment, particularly if your symptoms are mild. Most times, you would no longer find the need for drug-based medication.

If you have started your drug-based medication, consider the following as your options:

Consult your physician if you are planning to take natural dietary or herbal supplements just to make sure there will be no conflict with your prescription medicines.

Wean from drug-based medication by focusing on natural remedies, i.e. lifestyle adjustments as your primary therapeutic treatment.

Here are the basic natural remedies for bipolar:

Lifestyle Adjustments

Making healthy changes in your lifestyle prove to be an effective treatment to stabilize and normalize your mood. Here are essential ways to adjust your lifestyle and introduce healthy changes:

Increase your physical activity, but do the things that you will love doing. Living a sedentary life can trigger your depressive episode. Find things that you like and will allow you to move your body. Incorporate these activities in your routine.

For instance, if you love dancing, make it a point to spend an hour each day, at least three days in a week, to dance. If you enjoy walking you dog, do this three times a week initially, and then increase the frequency to five times a week, until you can do it every day. Spend 20 to 30 minutes each day for this activity.

Get adequate rest and sleep. You might be familiar with the powerful tandem of diet and exercise as a basic resolution for practically all illnesses. Do you know, however, that there is a third element? This is sleep, the phase where your body recovers from the stress and rigors of the day and restores its optimal function.

The problem is bipolar people find it difficult to sleep during their episodes. If you are in your manic episode, you are most likely to be awake and will find it difficult to fall asleep. If you are in your depressive episode, it is either you will hardly fall asleep, or you will find yourself sleeping excessively.

To get adequate sleep and rest, here are some of the things you can do without having to pop the pill:

☐ Make your bedroom conducive for sleeping. Remove all distractions and see to it that it is a place that will make you rest your mind and body to fall asleep.

☐ Establish a pattern for sleeping. For instance, set your own curfew for hitting the bed, say at 8:00 p.m. every night. Do your best to follow your schedule until this becomes a part of your routine and a good habit to keep.

Dietary Changes

Another crucial area where you can introduce changes and treat bipolar is your diet. While an anti-bipolar diet does not exist, making good food choices will certainly contribute much in stabilizing your mood.

A high-nutrient density diet is favorable to bipolar people. Make sure that your diet consists of healthy and nutritious food, specifically recipes that use natural and organic ingredients.

Avoid consumption of processed, instant and junk food as they contain chemicals that can interfere with your brain functions. Fruits and vegetables are your best bet when it comes to healthy eating, but make sure they are fresh and free from pesticide residues.

Chapter 4: When To See A Doctor?

Given the list of signs and symptoms, more or less you can assess for yourself if there is something wrong or if you suspect that you have bipolar disorder. If you feel like you have this problem, it is better to consult your doctor right away. Unfortunately, there are some who would tend to leave things as they are even if they know something is wrong. Some would even deny that they are manifesting the signs and symptoms of bipolar disorder.

It is a wrong misconception that bipolar disorder will get better on its own and that you do not need treatment. In fact, there are a lot of people manifests extreme moods and mood swings that would just neglect it and will think that it is normal. Many fail to notice that they already have signs and symptoms. Failure to act and to address the problem can only cause instability not just for yourself but as well as for other people. To avoid experiencing more problems and serious consequences later on, it is important that you consult a doctor now.

To keep your moods intact, it is essential that you get a treatment from a reliable and certified mental health provider. These experts have extensive experience in handling patients who have bipolar disorder. As such, you can have your symptoms under control.

If you are still hesitant undergo a treatment, you can always talk to a close friend to confide your worries and concern. You can also contact your trusted healthcare professional or any other person you are comfortable with and you trust. At least, you are on your way to taking the first step. Keep in mind that the first step will always be difficult. But once you get the necessary treatment or the prescribed medication, you can avoid worse manic episodes.

What to Do if You Have Suicidal Thoughts

People with bipolar disorder may experience having suicidal thoughts and risky behavior. When a person is already having these kinds of thoughts in mind, it can be really dangerous especially since they tend to be really emotional and irrational. These are usually common. So, if you are experiencing this situation or you know someone who does, doing the following is important:

Contact a friend or a family member

Contact and seek professional help from your trusted doctor

Call a suicide hot line number. In the United States, you can contact the toll-free hotline number of the National Suicide Prevention Lifeline at 800-8255.

For emergency help, contact 911 in the event that you may attempt suicide or if you have a loved one who is hurt.

Chapter 5: What Bipolar Disorder Is Not

For people to get the appropriate treatment, bipolar disorder may need to be differentiated from the signs and symptoms that are similar to it. We should note that not all mood swings are bipolar, and most people will have good and bad days. These can sometimes happen as a response to the ups and downs of life, but other times, you can just "wake up the wrong side of the bed." Some mood swings that are not part of bipolar disorder and can happen to anyone are understandable reactions to an unfortunate occurrence or reactions that are not particularly intense, noticeable, distressing or disruptive. Manic, hypomanic, or mixed episodes differentiate bipolar disorder from unipolar depression. Bipolar disorder can also be mistaken for illnesses that involve psychosis, such as schizophrenia. Schizophrenia involves episodes of prominent psychotic symptoms, such as hallucinations, delusions and disordered thinking but instead of experiencing intense moods, blunted moods accompany schizophrenia. Although individuals with schizophrenia may develop depression, unlike bipolar disorder, psychotic symptoms do not occur only in the presence of a depressed, manic, or hypomanic episode.

Bipolar disorder is often confused with schizoaffective disorder, which is another illness that includes both psychotic and mood symptoms. The major difference is that in bipolar disorder, psychotic symptoms only occur when there's mood symptoms, whereas, in schizoaffective disorder, psychotic symptoms are seen both when mood symptoms are present and when there are no mood symptoms for at least two weeks.

Mood swings are a common phenomenon in borderline personality disorder, but compared to bipolar disorder, they don't usually last as long and are not as marked as the moods in bipolar disorder. In borderline personality, mood swings happen as a reaction to events and are linked to certain personality characteristics.

Some states temporarily caused by taking certain illicit drugs may imitate episodes of bipolar disorder, but the effects of intoxication wear off quite rapidly and do not make up bipolar disorder. The symptoms of particular medical conditions like multiple sclerosis or hypothyroidism can also imitate bipolar disorder. And for this, accurate diagnosis of bipolar disorder is needed for proper treatment.

Signs and Symptoms

The basic symptoms of bipolar disorder are the periodic changes in mood, switching between periods of elevated mood, and periods of depression. If you are suffering from bipolar disorder, you may feel overly happy, energetic, even make reckless or impulsive decisions. During these manic episodes, you may feel a strong urge to cry, have feelings of hopelessness, and a negative attitude toward life. With hypomania - a less severe form of mania- generally, you feel pretty good and have a better sense of well-being.

An individual with bipolar disorder doesn't merely feel "down in the dumps;" their depressive state may cause them to have suicidal thoughts that alternate to feelings of endless energy and euphoria. These mood swings are extreme and can happen more frequently - every week or more sporadically, just twice a year. These mood swings have no defined pattern to them as one does not always happen before the other. Also, the length of time a state lasts varies, but luckily there are a number of treatments that can keep your moods under control, thereby enabling you live a productive life.

The typical onset of symptoms occur around 25 years of age, with the rates of bipolar disorder in men and women almost equal. Bipolar Disorder I has a feature of at least one manic episode, predated or followed by a major depressive episode. These manic episodes may be so severe that they may cause a break from reality or considerably hinder daily functioning. A person suffering from Bipolar I Disorder may need to be hospitalized.

People with Bipolar II Disorder may experience at least one major depressive episode, which may last two weeks or more and at least one hypomanic state lasting at least four days. But, they don't experience a manic episode. Cyclothymic disorder is distinguished by at least two years of multiple instances of hypomania and depressive symptoms – symptoms that are less severe than major depressive episodes and hypomanic episodes. During this period, symptoms show themselves at least half of the time and remain constant for two months at least. There are various stages of bipolar disorder, so the signs and symptoms differ from one person to another and from type to type. Below are the most common indications and symptoms of the emotional state of bipolar disorder.

Manic Symptoms

According to the DSM-5, a manic episode is a distinct and abnormal state of elevated, extensive or irritable mood spanning for at least a duration of one week while a hypomanic episode is characterized by a distinct and abnormal state of elevated, extensive, or irritable mood that lasts for a duration of at least four consecutive days.

During a manic episode, an individual who has been diagnosed with bipolar disorder may experience any of these signs and symptoms:

An extended period of an overly elated, happy, and outgoing mood - feeling high.

Restlessness

Being easily distracted

Feeling extremely irritable

Thoughts racing through the mind

Jumping from one thought to another when talking

Talking very fast

Taking on a lot of new projects

Little sleep

Boundless energy

An unrealistic confidence that you can do something

Making impulsive, pleasurable, and high-risk decisions such as shopping sprees, poor financial investments, sexual indiscretions, etc.

Increased agitation

High sex drive

Inflated self-esteem

Feelings of grandiosity

Increased goal-directed activity

Detachment from reality - may include delusions or hallucinations

Making grand and unattainable plans

Manic behaviors disrupt normal functioning at school or work, in relationships, social situations. Note that these behaviors are not as a result of a medical illness, alcohol or drug use, or a side effect of a drug.

Depressive Symptoms

The depressive side of bipolar disorder is defined by a major depressive episode, which causes a loss of interest or pleasure in life or a depressed mood. People with bipolar disorder may experience some of the following signs and symptoms during depressive states:

Feeling hopeless, tearful, sad , or empty for a major part of the day every day

Weight fluctuations - considerable weight loss or weight gain

Deriving no pleasure or interest in daily activities

Indecisiveness

Sleep disturbances - oversleeping or insomnia

Restlessness or dullness

Inability to concentrate

Suicidal attempts, thoughts, or plans

Feeling guilty and worthless

Feelings of fatigue

Loss of energy

Psychosis - a detachment from reality; delusions or hallucinations

Loss of interest in activities once enjoyed

Uncontrollable crying

Anxiety

Chapter 6: Mania: What It Is And How To Spot It

Mania, or manic episodes, are often described as the experience of an extreme high. While "high" connotes positivity, manic episodes are quite the contrary. Many individuals liken this emotional state to being in overdrive, where everything is heightened and one is in a constant state of agitation or feeling "wired".

Manic episodes take place when three or more symptoms listed below are experienced daily for at least a week:

-Extreme happiness, excitement, positivity, hopefulness, or joyfulness; often uncontrollable despite different stimuli

-Sudden and rapid crashes or changes in mood (e.g. from extreme positivity to anger, aggression, or irritability)

-Uncontrollable hyperactivity, restlessness, and agitation

-Unusually high energy levels

-Decreased urge/need to sleep; consequently, sleep patterns are disrupted and periods of wakefulness are extended

-Lack of concentration

-Complaints of having racing thoughts/flight of ideas

-Tendencies to create and believe in grandiose ideas that are impractical/unrealistic. In some cases, some develop unrealistic beliefs about themselves, such as the belief in their own "supernatural" powers and abilities, etc.

-Displaying poor judgment and indecision; impulsiveness

-Engaging in risky behaviour and activities; exaggerated sexual behaviour and an increased urge for sexual activity

If you notice these symptoms in your loved ones, it's important that you bring their attention to it. Most likely, their doctors have discussed strategies that they can employ for times such as these. So, a great way you can help is to assist them in monitoring their mood changes.

Chapter 7: Treating Borderline Personality Disorder

A diagnosis may be shocking, disappointing, or disturbing for borderline personality disorder. But BPD reacts positively to treatment, despite the impact it can have on a person's life. Those who suffer should expect permanent relief if they come out of the shadows to seek help. Psychotherapy, which is usually complemented by a combination of medication, skills education, and holistic healing techniques, restores wellness and vitality, is the cornerstone of BPD treatment plans.

Getting a Diagnosis

A borderline personality disorder (BPD) diagnosis can be a tricky proposition for professionals of mental health. Its symptoms partially overlap with other mental illness; its prevalence has long since been underestimated and often develops in the presence of similar or conflicting symptoms that can complicate diagnosis.

However, once an accurate diagnosis for BPD has been made, there are excellent opportunities for recovery. BPD patients looking for professional help will have access with a proven record of success to specialist therapies and other treatment methods.

BPD Treatment Program

Until care starts for borderline personality disorder, a medical specialist will be appointed to oversee and co-ordinate the overall patient rehabilitation program. Objectives or goals are generated to encourage the patient to ensure a consistent recovery rate. Healing programs are adapted to incorporate new approaches or strategies when there are or are no progress.

Although individuals are different, the overall structure of a BPD recovery plan generally contains the following essential characteristics:

• Individual, group, and family psychotherapy. Drug-centered care has become the norm for many forms of mental illness, with the support of therapy. But the equation is reversed with BPD. Therapy is still the core of all BPD treatment plans, and unique therapeutic approaches to cope with the singular symptoms of this surprisingly common condition have been developed.

• Medication. There are no medicines specifically designed for borderline personality disorders. Nevertheless, prescription drugs continue to be available to help improve the effects or underlying conditions of BPD.

• Life skills training and education. Classroom sessions that provide patients with information on the specifics of their mental health disorders and teaching them how to handle symptoms and related life complications have now become standard in the treatment of mental health regimes.

• Holistic methods of healing. Included in addition to more traditional therapy styles, holistic mind-body techniques are useful to patients with BPD for two reasons— firstly because they help reduce stress; and secondly, because they can help people to develop more self-control and self-control.

• Additional treatment services for health disorders co-occurring. If other mental health problems or drug use disorders are diagnosed, treatment programs must address these problems simultaneously with their attention to BPD symptoms.

Persons with a borderline suicidal personality disorder may be forced to be hospitalized in psychiatric care until the crisis passes or suffer from severe episodes of dissociative symptoms.

Different Types of Therapy for Bipolar Personality Disorder (BPD)

Psychotherapy is a core of a borderline personality disorder healthcare program in both outpatients and inpatients. The majority of men and women seeking BPD care will receive patient, community, and family counseling, with regular sessions where required.

While every one of them has several peculiar variations, at least one or two types of psychotherapy are part of the most popular treatment plans:

- Dialectic Behavioural Therapy (DBT)

Considering the gold standard in BPD therapy, DBT was mainly designed to treat this condition. This therapy teaches skills in emotional regulation, stress management, attention and self-confidence and interpersonal communication with practical guidance focusing on overall health and quality of life.

- Mentalization-Based Therapy (MBT)

The mentalization-based therapy is designed to enhance the ability of BPD sufferers to interpret their feelings and behavior with specific mental states not only in themselves but in others. Another treatment that is designed for BPD patients. With this knowledge in hand, patients can start to understand their condition as a prelude to their eventual recovery.

- Cognitive Behavioral Therapy (CBT)

Cognitive-behavioral therapy is a crucial component of most treatment procedures for mental health, including those which provide help to people with this disorder. In the course of CBT sessions, patients are taught to convert negative patterns of thinking into more positive and constructive states of mind until these habits are established.

- Eye-Movement Desensitization and Reprocessing (EMDR)

Through physical movement and mental focus, EMDR therapy enables patients with mental health problems to handle previous traumas safely and in an environment that focuses entirely on health and recuperation.

- Transference-Focused-Psychotherapy (TFP)

Here, the focus or attention is on building a positive, sympathetic relationship between the patient and the therapist, then serving as a model for the patient's behavioral and psychological reconstruction.

- Schema-Focused-Psychotherapy (SFT)

The original form of psychotherapy helps patients deal with their problems by alternating among five modes or regimes that define the BPD patient's underlying personality (according to SFT theory):

abandoned and confused babies, aggrieved and impulsive children, the unconditional protector, punitive parents, and healthy adults.

- Systems-Training-For-Emotional-Predictability and Problem-Solving (STEPPS)

This is a 20-week outpatient group therapy initiative that combines cognitive-behavioral restructuring and training in practice-oriented skills. The training sessions include family members and friends to help BPD sufferers develop a strong network of helpers and caregivers.

- Family Psycho-education

This therapy provides the loved ones of BPD patients with guidance, information, and emotional support to their advantage and to ensure their full co-operation in the disorder recovery program.

-   Additional Therapies For Co-Occurring Disorders

If co-occurring disorders are diagnosed, treatment is also necessary. Integrated mental or behavioral health treatment programs are designed specifically for managing multiple disorders simultaneously, and the majority of therapies within a standard BPD treatment program can be adequately adapted to deal with other mental health problems.

BPD MEDICATIONS

No specially developed drugs for the treatment of borderline personality disorder. Two pharmaceutical classes are, however, capable of fighting the most disabling BPD symptoms: mood stabilizers and anti-psychotics.

Anti-psychotics: These are usually prescribed for schizophrenia, but when administered in lower doses, the intensity of the cognitive and perceptual distortions which BPD patients often experience can be reduced. Extreme thoughts, paranoia, and dissociative episodes can substantially disrupt men's and women's lives, but anti-psychotics can assist them in managing those symptoms and reconnecting with realities.

Mood stabilizers: These are the medicine of choice for BPD people who fight impulsivity and are emotionally exposed. They can contribute to reducing the intensity of BPD explosive anger individuals and can counter the disabling anxiety, which is so often a partner of this all-encompassing mental health disorder.

Skills Training, Holistic Healing Process, and Education

Most BPD sufferers profit from advanced skill training programs that teach them the strategies to deal with the symptom of BPD. Having self-management skills are essential for the safety and well-being of people with mental health problems because the drugs do not always function, and therapists are not available 24 hours a day outside of the residential treatment facility.

In the meantime, information classes can help those with limited personality disorders gain an understanding of their conditions, clarifying misconceptions that may prevent them from committing themselves to recovery. However, the knowledge they gain about BPD can help them in the early stage to recognize symptoms and provide them with a much better idea of where they stand on the continuum of borderline personality disorders.

In residential mental health centers, holistic mental-body healing methods are routinely available today and may undoubtedly be of benefit to individuals with BPD during ambulatory programs. People with this disorder have difficulty managing their emotions, and holistic practices are designed to deal with this precise problem.

Listed below are some of the productive mind and body healing strategies for people with mental health disorder:

• Acupuncture

• Yoga

• Meditation

• Art or Music Therapy

• Equine therapy

• Tai Chi

- Massage therapy

- Nutritional therapy

Holistic treatment approaches tend to improve the health of people suffering from the BPD and not only from diseases, as they re-energetic their minds, bodies, etc.

Inpatient Treatment for Borderline Personality Disorder (BPD)

In clinics, 10 percent of those in outpatient treatment and up to 20 percent of those who receive residential treatment. The latter figures are remarkable as they demonstrate the awareness of mental health professionals that inpatient treatment facilities are essential in the initial phases of rehabilitation of BPD patients.

If people with limited personality disorder are diligent and committed to outpatient treatment, they are given a real opportunity to achieve a long-term symptom-free condition. But to ensure the best outcomes, the wisest way to start rehabilitation in a residential treatment facility for most BPD patients. How you learn in stay care will remain with you after you return to your life and equally provide you with a strong foundation to build on as soon as you move to a less rigorous ambulatory program.

Generally, the future following diagnosis is fantastic for men and women with BPD, which testifies to how much the field of mental health has benefited from this historically misunderstood disorder.

USING COGNITIVE BEHAVIORAL THERAPY IN TREATING BPD

CBT is a form of psychotherapy that may be used to deal with depressive disorder. CBT is a type of psychotherapy.

One-on-one consultation with a therapist can require psychotherapy. It can also involve group sessions with the therapist and other people with similar problems.

Although many strategies differ, they all help patients control their emotions, beliefs, and behaviors. Psychotherapy is also a forum for positive solutions to problems.

How Does CBT Fit Into Your Treatment?

Typically, a combination of medicine and psychotherapy is the primary treatment for bipolar disorder. CBT is one of the most common psychotherapy forms.

CBT can be used in several ways, and this includes:

• Managing the mental health symptoms

• Avoidance of behaviors which might lead to a re-emergence with these symptoms

• Learning effective coping techniques to help reduce feelings and stress

• Serving as an optional treatment when drugs are unsuccessful or are not an option.

How Does CBT Work?

The main objective of CBT is to help you gain a new perspective on your situation. It does so by questioning negative ideas and fears explicitly and helping you to manage or remove them.

Typically, the treatment is short term and focuses primarily on the elimination or control of specific problems. This includes your and the therapist's efforts.

You and the therapist should work together on the following during a CBT session:

Determine the issue Mental illness, job, stress, or anything else that may disturb you may be.

Examine the behaviors, emotions, and thoughts associated with BPD

Once you have established the problems, you can begin to work with the therapist to see how you respond to them.

Find negative or imprecise feelings, actions, and emotions

There are several ways to interpret or cope with a problem that makes the problem worse. This can include negative thinking about yourself or dwelling on the negative aspects of a circumstance or case.

Change your approach to personal problems.

Both and the therapist work together to replace the negative thoughts with more positive and constructive ones during a session. This can include a positive thought of your ability to cope and a more objective view of the situation.

Who Can Take CBT?

Cognitive-behavioral therapy in almost all cases can be successful. In a couple of settings, including hospitals and private practices, psychotherapy can be obtained. This is one of the most common therapy forms. Most employers offer psychotherapy through their employee support programs.

What Are The Adverse Effects?

Psychotherapy has no overt physical side effects. Furthermore, if you decide to try CBT, you will freely talk to a therapist or even a group of people about your problems. This can be frustrating and difficult to overcome.

CBT is a common therapy for a wide range of issues, including bipolar disorder management. The aim of the therapy is to recognize the concerns and responses to them. It then decides which reactions are toxic and substitutes for them with healthier alternatives.

Chapter 8: Myths & Facts On Bipolar Disorder

Those less sensitive or knowledgeable about bipolar disorder may indulge and believe in the common myths about bipolar disorder.   These individuals are only showing how little they know about bipolar disorder, and they should not be someone you need to go to in order to figure out if bipolar disorder is something that you are suffering from. Here are some common myths and facts about bipolar disorder that are floating

around today.
Myth: "People with bipolar disorder are crazy, and they constantly swing in and out of depression and mania."

Fact: Most people that suffer from bipolar disorder are more depressed than manic. If manic episodes do occur, they may be very minor and will go unnoticed. Most individuals will go for extended periods (days, moths, years, etc.) without ever showing any symptoms or experiencing any episodes.
Myth: "Bipolar disorder is uncontrollable without medication. Medication is your only hope to keep your bipolar disorder under control."

Fact: Even though medication is one of the best treatments for bipolar disorder there are other sources for treating this illness, and can help you cope with things a lot better.

A healthy diet, ample sleep, routine exercise, therapy, and self-help methods will help you cope with things better, and may even assist you in beating your bout with bipolar disorder.
Myth: "You will not be able to live a happy and normal life with bipolar disorder."

Fact: Individuals that suffer from bipolar disorder often maintain great careers, healthy relationships, and happy families. Even though living with bipolar disorder will bring a number of difficulties, it is important to always know that you can overcome them by taking them on fearlessly and leaning on your support system when you need to.
Myth: "Bipolar disorder only has an effect on your mood."

Fact:
Even though there are some at-home tests that do exists, bipolar disorder is mostly

genetic.

And the test only has the ability to tell you if your genetics put you at a higher risk for developing or having bipolar disorder. The best way to find out if you have bipolar disorder is to talk to your doctor. Your doctor will be able to help you sort things out better, and will assist you in identifying and maybe even debunking your suspected symptoms.

Myth: "There is a way to be tested for bipolar disorder. So, you should definitely go get tested.

Fact: Most people have this perception that bipolar disorder is only about constant mood swings, depression, and acts of mania. However, bipolar disorder affects your libido, memory, concentration, energy, self-esteem, and appetite. Bipolar disorder has the ability to bring a number of health problems like, high blood pressure, heart disease,

diabetes, anxiety, and migraines.
Myth:
"Bipolar disorder is only a made-up condition. It's not real."

Fact:
Bipolar disorder is an illness. Those that take this disorder lightly are not aware that it is treatable, and that recovery from it will take a lot of work, time, and honest effort. Bipolar disorder should not be considered something that should be ignored, because if left untreated people could end up getting hurt physically, emotionally, mentally, or a combination of all three.
Myth:
"Children cannot have bipolar disorder. That's impossible!

Fact:
Symptoms of bipolar disorder can affect children as early as six years old. Children

with bipolar disorder tend to have parents that have the condition, and can have intense mood swings or shifts between mania and depression.

Myth:
"You will become dependent on your bipolar medications, and you will not be as sober as you should be."

Fact:
Even though it is possible to develop a dependency on medications, it will be highly impossible if you take the medication as directed and prescribed. The medications are meant to stabilize your moods. If you decide to take medications to treat bipolar disorder, it always best to use as directed.

Myth:
"Therapy will not work. It's only a bunch of moaning and crying. So, how can it help you with such a serious condition as

bipolar   disorder?"
Fact:
Therapy has been tested and proven to be and effective method in treating bipolar disorder. Talking to people really helps. Talk therapy can help you identify the triggers of your behavior and can assist you in taking effective measures to treat yourself.

Myth:
"Treatment are for people who are too lazy and weak to deal with their problems on   their   own."
Fact:
Seeking treatment is a huge step and take a   great   amount   of   courage. You are not weak if you go out to seek treatment, you are only making yourself stronger by facing the fact that you have bipolar disorder and going outside of yourself for help. Seeking treatment and the guidance of others can be very

beneficial to those who feel like or who
have   bipolar   disorder.

Chapter 9: Adjusting Of Lifestyle

The second part of the equation includes changes, sometimes significant, to your lifestyle. It may be boring to hear that after every kind of problem you will have to adjust your diet and change your habits, but as already said, you have to want to get better and that's the way to do it.

In this case it is not so much a matter of what to include in your dietary habits. It is mostly a matter of what to avoid as it contributes to the remedy of your condition. This is a list of what to include and what to avoid:

1) Omega 3 acids

Otherwise known as fish oil. It is one of the few foods that if you are suffering from bipolar disorder, you should consume on a daily basis. It improves the functionality of your brain and decreases the appearance of manic episodes. What to consume? Tuna, herring, mackerel, salmon and trout.

2) Western style diet

This is what to avoid or moderate. A diet rich in red meat, fats, trans fats and carbohydrates. This kind of food habit has been held responsible for a lot of diseases and in general it is considered as a"problematic"diet, though not directly linked with bipolar disorder.

Moderation would not exclude these foods from you diet. It would required that you consume less quantities of it and add foods of less saturated fats and carbohydrates.

3) Balanced diet

The human body needs to receive nutrients that come from all kinds of foods. Therefore, you need to include fresh fruit, vegetables, grains, low-fat dairy, lean meat, nuts and seeds. These foods will maintain a healthy body which will be able to resist much more to any kind of disease including bipolar disorder.

You may also be bored of listening that you should add exercise to your everyday life. The same statement still holds true. You need to want to get better. And in this case it is what the doctor ordered.

Exercise makes you feel good even if you are in perfect health, let alone suffering from any kind of condition. Keep in mind that if you choose to rely solely on traditional medicinal compounds, some of them entail a side-effect of making you gain weight. And while your mood may improve, your body will deteriorate.

For those that like variety in their lifestyle the news are bad. If you are a person who likes changes and surprises and you are suffering from bipolar disorder you need to change your everyday life into a routine. Changes and especially important ones will trigger your disorder. You need to avoid exposing yourself to situation like occupational changes, relationship changes and any other form of change that will contribute to a possible relapse of your condition.

You may include a lot of things in your routine so that life is not boring, but you need to make it a routine. Otherwise the equation will not reach the desired result.

Chapter 10: Diagnosis Of The Disorder

One of the hardest things to do with this kind of disorder is to diagnose it. Most of the people who have it are not going to want to have anything to do with the doctor or psychiatrist who is trying to help them out and so they are going to ignore them and not take the help. Often it is going to take family members to see the issue and initiate the help that is needed before the person with the disorder is going to get the help. They are not going to go in on their own because they are not going to see that they have any issues at all.

Once you can get the person with the disorder to come into the door, the diagnosis of this disorder is going to be based on the assessment that is done in the clinic by a professional of mental health. The best way to do this is to present the different criteria of the disorder to the patient, these criteria are listed above, and ask them if they think that any of these describe them. This is going to get the participant involved in the cure, making it more likely to work. Plus, a doctor is usually not going to have enough time or outside experience with the patient to determine on their own if the characteristics are there and this can provide them with a usually truthful means of getting to it.

When you allow the person who has this kind of disorder to actively help with the diagnosis, they are going to be more willing to get the help that the professional is going to get them. There are some clinicians though who decide that it is best to not tell their patients that they have this diagnosis because they believe that it is full of stigma and the person will be against the treatment because they may have heard in the past that this is an untreatable disorder. While this is one way to go, there is a lot of research to show that the person suffering from the disease should know about it to get the most effective treatment that is possible.

During this evaluation, the patient is going to be asked a lot of questions about their symptoms including when they began and how severe they were. The might also be asked some questions that relate to how these symptoms are impacting their life. Some of the issues that the doctor is going to take special notes about would be any thoughts that are about harming others, experiences with doing self-harm, and any thoughts of suicide that the person has.

The diagnosis is going to be based on what the patient has been reporting at sessions as well as what the doctor has been able to observe in their short time. These two things are usually going to be able to combine to give a good outlook on what is going on. There are a few other tests that can be done to help determine if borderline personality disorder is present in the person. Sometimes some laboratory tests or a physical exam are going to be done to help rule out some of the other things that might trigger these symptoms, such as the person abusing substances or a thyroid condition; both of which could cause some of the same behaviors as what is find in borderline personality disorder.

Once the disorder has been determined and diagnosed in a patient, it is time to get to work with giving them the treatment that they need to stay healthy and get their lives back. While this is going to be a lot of work and will take some time, it is something that must be done if the person wants to get their life back and be much happier. Here is some more information about how the disorder could be diagnosed and how the person should get the help that they need to start feeling better in no time.

International Classifications

There are a few classifications that you will be able to find that are used internationally to help make the diagnosis. These classifications can be nice because they allow the clinician to be able to do the diagnosis without having to go on their own personal beliefs and can keep everything organized and the same throughout. The idea of borderline personality disorder, is one that is recognized by the World Health Organization. It is then divided into two other categories which will be discussed a bit below.

Impulsive Type

The first kind of category that is recognized in this is the impulsive type. Out of the things that are discussed below, at least three of them need to be present to diagnose someone with this category of the disorder.

A marked tendency to get out of control or to act out. This is going to happen unexpectedly and will not be due to someone causing the issue or forcing them to act out. Often the act is going to be done by the person without them worrying or even thinking about the consequences that could happen with their action. This is just something that they are going to do, perhaps over a slight disagreement or other issue, that should not have been that big of a deal but which was turned into one.

A marked tendency of the sufferer to get into behavior that is considered quarrelsome and they are going to have a lot of conflicts with the others around them. This is especially going to be true with impulsive acts that have been criticized or thwarted. This is a person who is routinely getting into fights with others around them and who see any little slight as an excuse to get in a big fight together.

A liability to having strong outbursts when it comes to violence or anger. Not only are they having these issues, but they do not have the ability that is needed to control the explosions or other issues that come up. They will seem very angry but they will also seem like they do not have the means to come back down and be calm again even if they had wanted.

These people are also going to have some difficulty in staying with their course of action if they are not able to get a reward right away. They may have been really interested in doing it, but when it did not provide the immediate reward that they were looking for, they most likely became upset and angry and so decided to just give up on it. This is something that would happen quite often and the person would only stick with things they know they can finish and be rewarded with.

These people will often have capricious and unstable moods that can change almost without any warning. It might be hard to keep up with these kinds of people.

These are the five criteria that will often be found in someone who is dealing with the impulsive kind of this disorder. You are going to notice that they are going to do things often without any thought to what they are doing or what is going to happen

92

when they are done, and this can be a dangerous thing. For a person to be diagnosed with this kind of disorder, they are going to need to have at least three of the things mentioned above present when they talk to their therapist in the office.

Borderline Type

Next comes the borderline type. This one is going to be a little bit different. This is going to take a bit from the list above and then adds in a bit from the list that is going to be presented below. You will need to have a minimum of three of those symptoms that are found for the impulsive type present as well as a minimum of 2 of the ones below to get a diagnosis of this category. Some of the things to look for include:

A person with this type would often have some uncertainty and disturbances in their self-image as well as their internal preferences and their aims in life. They do not think that they are worth much and even though they crave interaction with others, they are not sure why these others would want to have anything to do with them. They may wonder around a lot looking confused because they do not know who they are, what they should do with their lives, or what is to become of them.

They might also have a higher liability to get involved in relationships that are often unstable and intense. This might include those whirlwind relationships where they meet and get married in just a few short months, but it does not have to be this severe either to fit. Since the relationship is so unstable it is not going to last and since it was intense, it is likely to cause a sort of emotional crisis in the person who is suffering from the disorder.

These people are going to show really excessive efforts to never become abandoned. They are scared that one day they will wake up and not have anyone around to be their friends or to help them out when they need. This is further complicated by the fact that they are pushing others away and are not very good at seeing other's points of view. They are going to work almost obsessively to make sure that others do not leave them alone so that they can always have the help and companionship that they are looking for.

They are also going to have frequent threats as well as acts of self-harm. This is often not in an attempt to get someone to act the way that they would like or to change the feelings of someone else. This is more of something that they do in the hopes of getting their own emotions in check. They are going to have a lot of trouble with their own emotions and since they are not able to keep them under control, they may turn to self-harm in the hopes of getting some relief.

Frequent feelings that surround them of emptiness. Because they do not have any plans for their future or for the things that they want to do in their lives, they are going to feel empty. They do not have any goals or long term plans, so often they are just going to wander around and hope that things work out the best. This can lead to a life that is pretty empty.

They are going to often demonstrate behavior that is impulsive. This is going to include things such as substance abuse and speeding. The idea behind doing these things is because it gives the sufferer a bit of a break for the bad feelings or uncontrolled emotions that they are going through so that they can just feel better for a bit. The issue comes when the person begins to feel a bit guilty about their behavior and so they will feel even worse than they did before.

As mentioned before, there needs to be quite a few things that are present before someone is going to be diagnosed with this form of the disorder. But those who meet these requirements should get the help that they need as soon as possible.

Millon's Subtypes

First we are going to take a look at the different subtypes that are used when it comes to borderline personality disorder. Theodore Millon has in the past proposed that there are four different subtypes when it comes to borderline personality disorder. Within these different categories, a person who has this disorder is going to exhibit usually one of more of the following things (these include the subtypes of the person with borderline personality disorder as well as the features that come with it):

Discouraged—this subtype is also going to include the features of someone who is avoidant. You will find that a person who fits into this category is powerless, helpless, depressed, feels like there is no hope for them or their live, feels like they are in a constant jeopardy and vulnerable, humble, loyal, submissive, and pliant.

Petulant—this category is also going to include the features of someone who is very negative about the thing that are going on around them. You will find that a person who fits into this category is quickly disillusioned and that they can be slighted at a moment's notice, resentful, pessimistic, sullen, defiant and really stubborn to get along with, restless, impatient, and very negative about everything.

Impulsive—this category is also going to include the features of someone who is very antisocial and does not want to be around others. Some of the features that you will find in a person who suffers from this include someone who is potentially suicidal, someone who is irritable, gloomy, and can become agitated on occasion. These people are going to be fearful of losing things and are frenetic, distractible, flighty, superficial, and capricious.

Self-destructive—this category is also going to include the features of someone is very masochistic or depressive. They are going to be really moody and high strung and these are going to show up more and more over time, they may think at times about suicide as an option many of their positive features are going to begin to deteriorate. They are deferential, conforming, and angry over little things, and will turn inwards to themselves rather than making friends.

It is possible for someone to fit into more than one of these categories and have this kind of disorder, but this kind of helps to divide out the different symptoms and make them make a bit more sense for those who are learning about them or diagnosing them.

The Conclusion

While there are a variety of different thoughts that come with this disorder, they all are pretty much going to work together to summarize what is going on with this disorder. It is not a simple one and there is not necessarily one definition that is going to be able to describe what is going on for each case. While some cases are going to have abuse in the past of the sufferer, not all of the cases will have had abuse and even if a person was abused in the past it does not mean that they are going to get this disorder. There are a lot of things that need to be in place for this issue to show up and it is complicated to take control of.

Even those who are trained to deal with this kind of condition are going to find that sometimes it is hard to diagnose it as the right personality disorder and sometimes it can be given the wrong diagnosis. This can be harmful to the sufferer because they are not going to be getting the help that they need at the right time. But the definitions that are given above are able to give a good starting point, as well as some experience and training, will help the professional to give the right diagnosis so the sufferer can get the help that they need.

Family Members

Even the way that the person with the disorder is treating the others who are around them can be a way of diagnosing them. People who have this disorder are going to be much more prone to disliking their family members and they are often going to be angry at these same people. Often the person with the disorder is going to work to alienate themselves from the family because they are mad over some little slight or they are worried that the family members are going to become to see a problem. Often the family members are going to feel a bit helpless and angry about the way that they are relating with this person and may wonder what they can do to make things right again.

There was a study done in 2003 that found that the thoughts of the family members would change once they found out that the behavior was for a reason. In most cases, the anger and hurt towards the person with the disorder would go up once their family members began to understand what is going on. While this would not seem like something that would happen, it is often believed that these feelings are occurring because the family is being given the wrong kind of information about the disorder so they are blaming the person rather than the issue at hand.

The best way for family members to be able to help out the one that they love is to learn as much as possible about the disorder. It is easy to start looking through books and watching shows about the disorder and while this might be a good place to start in some cases, you will find that it is often the wrong information. Get out there and find the information that is the right information and this is going to help make more sense out of what you are seeing with your loved one.

This is going to be just as difficult for members of the family to handle as it is for the person who is going through the issue. They are the ones who have been emotionally harmed by their loved one not wanting to have anything to do with them. It is important that the family gets the therapy and help that they need to feel better about the situation. Understanding the whole situation and how it is affecting the family and the sufferer can make it easier to get through the whole situation together.

Adolescence

The onset of these symptoms of the disorder are usually going to happen sometime in adolescence or in young adulthood. In some cases, it is possible for the symptoms to occur in children, but this is not as prevalent. Symptoms that occur among a teenager is going to predict if borderline personality disorder is going to occur in their adult life. Some of the symptoms that can be present include severe shame, attempts to get in an exclusive relationship that often will not work out, self-injury that is not committing suicide, behavioral problems, being really sensitive to rejection, and severe issues with body image that go beyond what is normal for teenagers to feel.

It is discouraged to diagnose anyone who is younger than 18 with this disorder just because there are so many variables and mood changes in young adults and teenagers that it would be extremely easy to miss out or miss-diagnose someone who is just having their regular teenage concerns. This does not mean that the disorder cannot be diagnosed ahead of time, but it is usually dealt with in a case by case basis and most clinicians will not deal with at all until the person is 19. If it is diagnosed, the features will have to be present as well as consistent for a year or more before the diagnosis can be made.

If someone is diagnosed with this when they are a teenager, it is most likely going to predict that the person is going to have this same disorder when they are adults. Among those who were diagnosed with this disorder when they were younger, there is usually two groups; one is going to have the disorder and it is going to remain pretty stable over a period of time and then the other group that is going to have those who move in and also out of their diagnosis. An earlier diagnosis is sometimes helpful when trying to get an effective treatment plan in place, but since this kind of diagnosis is tricky, it is often not done. For those who are suffering from borderline personality disorder as teens, family therapy is usually the option that is the most preferred.

Diagnosing with Other Disorders

It is not uncommon for someone who is dealing with this kind of disorder to also have some other disorders, whether it is other personality disorders or something else, that are going to show up at the same time. This makes it even harder to find the personality disorder because it may be masked by some of the other symptoms that are there. Compared to those who have some of the other personality disorders, those who have borderline personality disorder are going to have a higher rate for also meeting the criteria for other disorders such as:

Mood disorders—this is going to include things like bipolar disorder and major depression

Anxiety disorders—there are a lot of these that can be met as well and would include post-traumatic stress disorder, social anxiety disorder, and panic disorder

Other kinds of personality disorder

Substance abuse

Eating disorders—this would include things like bulimia and anorexia nervosa

Attention deficit hyperactivity disorder

Somatoform disorders

Dissociative disorders

If a person with this personality disorder has one of these other issues, they should not be diagnosed with the personality disorder until that other issue has been dealt with. These other issues can give some of the same symptoms and sometimes taking care of these can be a simpler method of dealing with the personality disorder. This is unless the symptoms of the personality disorder can be proven to have been around for many years before the other issue came into play.

Also, it is more likely that women are going to experience some of the issues listed above while men will receive some of the others. For example, men are going to be higher with the substance use disorders while the women are going to have more of the eating disorders. It is important that you get these other disorders taken care of if you would like to see some of the best results with treating your borderline personality disorder. It is going to be pretty much impossible to take care of the personality disorder if you have some of the other issues listed above in the way because these are going to onset the disorder and will keep it going even with a lot of therapy in the process.

This is why most professionals will do a thorough examination of the patient to figure out if there are some other issues that are present in the patient. This can make it much easier to cure the personality disorder once the other issues are done. This can be done with some preliminary therapy or through the use of medications to treat issues such as like anxiety and depression for the best results.

Mood disorders

Many of those who suffer from this kind of disorder are also going to have some severe mood disorders. This is going to include things such as bipolar disorder and major depressive disorder. Some of the symptoms that come with borderline personality disorder are going to be similar to what you can find in mood disorders so this can make the diagnosis of the personality disorder difficult. It is very common for someone to get misdiagnosed; they will be told that they have bipolar disorder when they really have borderline personality disorder and it can go the other way as well.

For those who have bipolar disorder, they may have some of the symptoms of borderline personality disorder, but these symptoms are just going to appear while the person is going through one of their episodes and then they will go back to normal when the mood is stabilized. This is why it is so important that the clinician make sure that their client's mood is completely stable before they do their diagnosis.

For those who do not know much about either of the two disorders, they are going to look very much the same. Even some clinicians who study the two quite a bit are going to find that it is difficult, but there are a few differences that you can watch for that will help. First, the mood swings of the two are going to be different in their durations. For some people with bipolar, the episodes are going to last for a minimum of two weeks each time while the moods in someone with borderline personality disorder is going to last much less time. The mood switches in those with bipolar are going to take place over a series of days while the ones for BPD are going to change by the minute or hour.

Next, the moods that come with bipolar disorder are not going to be responding to changes that occur in the environment while the same is not true for borderline personality disorder. What this means is that for a person with bipolar disorder, their mood is not going to be lifted if there is a positive event in their lives while this kind of situation would have the potential to life the mood of someone with BPD. On the other hand, someone with bipolar disorder would not be brought down if they are really happy just because a bad event happens, but someone with BPD can easily be brought down at a moment's notice.

And then, when those with BPD are experiencing euphoria, they are going to do it without any racing thoughts and they are not going to have the need for less sleep. Often they are not going to have periods of sleep disturbance as well. On the other hand, those with bipolar are always going to have racing thoughts, trouble sleeping, and disturbances in their appetite.

This is why it is going to take some time for the clinician to determine if your loved one has a personality disorder or not. It is not as easy as it might look since there are some similarities in symptoms that the person is feeling and often they are just going to happen for different lengths or for different reasons. A thorough examination can help to determine if someone is suffering from true borderline personality disorder or if they are having issues with a mood disorder.

Premenstrual Dysphoric Disorder

Premenstrual Dysphoric Disorder, or PMDD, is a condition that can occur in some women and some of the symptoms are going to match up with what you can find in borderline personality disorder. It is estimated that between 3 and 8 percent of women are going to feel these symptoms and most of them are going to occur somewhere between 5 and 11 days before the period starts and then will go away after it has begun. There are quite a few symptoms that are similar to what you might find with borderline personality disorder and would include things like trouble with their relationships, difficulty with concentrating, binge eating, anxiety, and feeling like things are out of their control, feeling hopeless, depressed, irritability, and mood swings.

Most of the women who have PMDD will start to experience these kinds of symptoms when they are early on in their twenties, but it is often going to take them until they are in their thirties to get the treatment that they need. While some of the symptoms between BPD and PMDD are similar, they are two different things. They are going to be distinguished by the duration of the symptoms as well as the timing and the PMDD is not going to have issues with impulsivity.

Axis II Disorders

Over 66 percent of those who have borderline personality disorder are also going to have the right criteria for meeting another kind of personality disorder at some point during their lives. The most common would be the cluster a disorders like schizotypal, schizoid, and paranoid. The next common would be the cluster B disorders like narcissistic, histrionic, and antisocial disorders. In some cases they may have other issues such as obsessive compulsive disorder, dependent disorder, and avoidant disorder. These disorders could have occurred before the borderline personality disorder came about or they can show up afterwards during the treatment or a few years later.

The diagnosis of borderline personality can be difficult at times. If there are other underlying causes that are in the way, it can become difficult to determine what symptoms are from this personality disorder, and which come from the other issues that are present. Only a professional clinician will be able to determine if you or someone else has borderline personality disorder and the right steps that you will need to take to get the right treatment.

Chapter 11: Sex And Intimacy

Physical intimacy is a very important component of a healthy, loving relationship. The quality of such intimacy often reflects both the trust and emotional alliance of that partnership. For this reason, we often hear that most relationship problems can be found in the bedroom. While some people report that they can separate their sexual feelings from their emotional feelings, tension or conflict in a relationship frequently impacts both the frequency and quality of physical intimacy. Similarly, a person's self-image influences his capacity to freely and comfortably engage in sexual intimacy.

Being in a relationship with someone who has bipolar disorder presents challenges for emotional intimacy and the maintenance of a satisfying sexual relationship. The good news is that it is still possible to have a healthy sex life when loving someone with bipolar disorder.

All Relationships Have Sex/Intimacy Issues

Let's begin by placing your bond with your bipolar partner within the larger framework of relationships to see how these relationships are influenced by societal views regarding sex. As children we receive a wide range of messages about sex from our parents, relatives, religion, community, peers, and media. Many of the messages may seem confusing — and contradictory.

These guidelines often reflect mixed messages about what is sexually appropriate. Some religions emphasize procreation as the primary reason for sex and instill guilt for the pleasure we associate with sexual intimacy. We receive other messages that emphasize the importance of postponing sex until marriage, and still others that encourage young men to be sexually active as a way of proving their masculinity. If we pay attention to media reports, we would think that people are having sex everywhere and around-the-clock. By contrast, actual studies of sexual behavior suggest that while many people are leading a very active sex life, the numbers do not compare with what is depicted by the media.

The mixed messages we receive about sex as children serve to heighten our confusion about our sexuality as adults. It is no wonder that partaking in sexual intimacy provokes a wide range of expectations and emotions that foster or inhibit the development of healthy physical intimacy.

CASE STUDY: Richard and Pam

Richard and Pam's seven-year marriage showcases a number of complex issues that can arise regarding intimacy and sexuality in the bipolar relationship. Pam had known Richard for more than a year prior to their being married and was aware of his bipolar illness. The couple sought counseling after an escalation in Richard's sexual activities that undermined the sense of trust that Pam had worked hard to maintain. Although they experienced a very satisfactory and active sex life early in their relationship, the frequency and quality of physical intimacy had greatly diminished over the last several years. Pam had initiated couples counseling as a last resort to maintain their relationship.

To a great extent Pam blamed herself for the diminished interest in intimacy. However, as she came to understand, much of her decreased libido resulted from feelings of hurt and disappointment triggered by the feeling that Richard wasn't fully present for her. In part, this occurred because of Richard's bouts of mania and depression. Simultaneously he had seemed to distance himself from her, partly as a result of his difficulty with being assertive about many areas of their shared life. Since he was unable to state what he really wanted, Richard became resentful of Pam, which fueled her sense of rejection and their mutual withdrawal from each other.

Although he struggled to be faithful to Pam, Richard developed an interest in Internet pornography. Pam discovered this activity and, while she confronted him once, she soon accepted his actions and blamed herself for not being physically available to him. She rationalized that at least he wasn't having an affair, and she focused on the many positive aspects of their relationship. Still, Pam suffered a profound blow to her ego and a disappointment that triggered a growing sense of alienation.

Only after Pam discovered that her husband had sought contacts with women on the Internet did she become angry enough to threaten divorce if he did not accept individual and couples counseling. At first Richard minimized his activities by telling Pam that he only fantasized about contacting women. Then, he recanted and admitting to sexual contacts with several of the women, although he had not become romantically involved with any of them.

This pattern of dealing with issues of intimacy can occur in any relationship, but the quickness to act on sexual impulses is a major challenge for many individuals with bipolar disorder. It can be especially challenging when the nonbipolar partner behaves like Pam, fearful of conflict and feeling overly responsible for or overly understanding of her partner's behaviors. As an outcome of therapy, Richard and Pam became much more comfortable sharing their respective feelings. Richard made a commitment to the relationship, and Pam made the commitment to temporarily suspend any distrust while hoping they would reestablish their mutual faith.

Intimacy Does Not Always Equal Sex

A fulfilling sexual relationship can be a vital part of a healthy relationship. If you and your partner enjoy an active sex life despite the many distractions of everyday life, you are one of the fortunate ones. On the other hand, if competing demands on your life begin to interfere with your relationship, it may be time to reassess your priorities.

As a relationship evolves, the desire for sexual intimacy may vary, but it is only a problem when one partner desires intimacy more than the other. Too frequently couples become complacent and neglect to keep their sex life exciting. Other times, the pressure of parenthood causes problems. When a doting parent becomes overly focused on raising children, she may inadvertently neglect the romantic aspect of her relationship with her partner. For other partners, being part of a family may replace or compete with feeling fully comfortable with one's sexuality. You may soon experience a sense of familial connection like the one you experienced with your family of origin. A sense of family love soon dominates and distracts from the focus of any physical desire for intimacy.

Since differences in desire for sexual intimacy can lead to tension in a relationship, each couple must decide how best to address the issue. You may also want to engage the help of a marriage counselor or a sex therapist. It is important to remember that a couple can grow to value their relationship in many ways, and what works for one couple may not work for another. Even a hearty sex life may be based on a dysfunctional relationship, so sex alone is not the key to a successful bond.

Sex Does Not Always Equal Intimacy

People often forget that sex can be a way of avoiding intimacy. The classic story of the man who seeks sex with a prostitute to avoid the real issues at home with his wife is a good example. Some people shy away entirely from intimate relationships, preferring more casual associations and the one-night stand to satisfy their sexual urge.

ASK THE DOCTOR

How important is intimacy in my sex life?

During and after sex, do you feel closer to your partner? Or do you secretly wait for it to be over with, or wish it were happening some other way? Do you love your partner despite the way he performs in bed? Physical intimacy can take many forms and it is a vital part of a loving relationship. However, it can be most fulfilling when it is grounded in the emotional intimacy that allows each partner to be fully present with the other.

Some couples use sex as a way of making up after an argument. But sex alone is a poor substitute for conversation and will not reveal the root of their problem. Some couples come to expect this pattern and will pick a fight just to have sex as if their sexual intimacy serves to validate their partner's love. When sex is used as a form of reassurance for the partner who feels abandoned or is the target of her partner's anger, it camouflages a weakened relationship. Other couples may be going through the motions of sex because they feel they "must," but one or both parties are present in body only. Their minds are elsewhere, thinking about another person or some mundane chore they need to do on the following day.

Can you see how many people wrongly equate sex with intimacy and intimacy with sex? Even if your partner was not bipolar the two of you would still more than likely experience sexual issues.

Medications and Sex Drive

Some medications prescribed for bipolar illness can diminish both sexual desire and performance, and even those that don't may still adversely affect your bipolar partner in terms of his sexual appetite. Let's look at the big picture as far as medication is concerned:

· Given the complex interconnectedness of human physiology, it is possible for any drug (including alcohol) to have some impact on the user's performance or sexual appetite. Alcohol, for example, can lessen inhibitions, but it can also inhibit male potency.

· People who live with bipolar disorder are not the only ones who are prescribed antidepressants or other medications that inhibit sex drive. People take antidepressants for problems other than bipolar disorder.

· Not all people are adversely affected by the sexual side effects of a given medication, as no drug affects everyone the same way.

· A person's memory can be faulty or selective. Although medication can lead to sexual dysfunction, sometimes the user of a particular drug was already experiencing sexual issues before taking the drug in question.

· Antidepressants are not the only drugs that may cause sexual side effects. Some people are also affected by antipsychotic medication. Moreover, drugs prescribed for high blood pressure (antihypertensives) and high cholesterol have also been reported to reduce sexual desire and/or performance.

· The aging factor has a debilitating effect on sexual performance and desire. We are not implying that seniors no longer seek or enjoy sex, but everyone experiences a normal decrease in sexual activity as they age. A woman reaches her sexual peak during her middle twenties and experiences the earliest changes of her libido (sex drive) at midlife. The male libido peaks at age eighteen and begins its decline after age forty-five, the time when a man's level of testosterone begins to decrease. However, some seniors experience diminished interest because they feel inadequate and less sexually appealing then they were at an earlier age. Discomfort with their changing bodies alters their self-image, which makes some people shun physical intimacy. For others, life experience and shifting priorities can also play a role.

If your bipolar partner does not seem to have a strong interest in physical intimacy, you may want to put it in perspective.

Many other factors besides the impact of medications may lead to a diminished sex drive.

Drugs to Increase Sexual Performance

The most common drugs prescribed for enhancing sexual performance and desire in men are Viagra, Cialis, and Levitra. However, since these drugs tend not to be covered by health insurance plans they can be very expensive. It's important that your doctor knows what other medications your partner is taking before a sexual enhancer is prescribed. These medications may have side effects and potentially negative interactions when combined with other medications.

Some men report that herbal remedies such as ginseng, horny goat, and yohimbe bark extract enhance their libido. Still, it should be emphasized that herbal remedies depend on their stimulating properties. Some preparations, like yohimbe bark extract, can induce high blood pressure and anxiety and, as a result, have become illegal in certain countries. Your bipolar partner should be wary of taking any substance that increases the potential for anxiety and should consult with his doctor before taking any herbal remedies.

WORD TO THE WISE

Enjoy Intimacy

Some people think of "sex" in terms of "orgasms." However, physical contact can still be mutually pleasurable and signal intimacy even with the failure to achieve orgasm. Kissing, touching, and caressing are also enjoyable and sexy.

For women, estrogen therapy is sometimes used to enhance sexual desire by increasing blood flow to the vagina. Progesterone can also be combined with the estrogen. Although women have lower amounts of testosterone than men, it is reported that testosterone plays a role in female sexual performance.

Since some people are uncomfortable discussing their concerns about sex with their physician, many are turning to the Internet for information about medications and herbal supplements. But, this can be harmful because of their potential negative side effects. Before beginning any new drug regimen, it is important that you and your partner openly discuss this with your doctor. Also, whether your partner is taking an over-the-counter herb or a prescription, it is advisable to have his blood pressure regularly checked since these treatments often work on the premise of stimulating the bloodstream. If your partner suffers from high blood pressure, he's less likely to be given a prescription drug of this type.

A wide variety of medications and alternative therapies is available today, and, since your relationship with a bipolar partner is not a unique phenomenon, several choices of treatment are available that can help increase your partner's sexual drive or performance. If affordable and your partner is able to take them, you may improve the satisfaction of your physical intimacy. But if these drugs are not an option, you may need to explore alternative forms of intimacy.

Other Factors

Some people feel that they must be in a particular frame of mind, or "in the mood," to have sex. The more diversions and responsibilities that we assume in our daily lives, the greater the demands that compete for our time. The desire for sex is diminished when other pursuits are prioritized. If you or your partner brings work home from the office, even mentally, your attention is otherwise diverted and you're less likely to be in the mood for sexual intimacy. If you work from home it can be difficult to switch gears from business matters to time spent alone with your partner. You may be mulling over some unresolved problem, or mentally planning your next day's schedule. Or, you and your partner may find yourselves talking in bed about the needs and activities of your children rather than sharing intimate moments together. Perhaps, by the time you begin preparing for bed, you're too fatigued for anything other than sleep.

During a manic episode your partner may have an increased sexual drive, but simultaneously her thoughts may be taking her in all different directions. Think about the last time you were disinterested in sex and had trouble falling asleep because you could not stop thinking about the kids or the checkbook or getting the car fixed; then, multiply the intensity of such rumination by ten. That is what goes on in your bipolar partner's head.

ASK THE DOCTOR

What are some chronic reasons for diminished sexual interest?

Other common causes for diminished sexual desire include anemia, diabetes, infections, a history of sexual abuse, conflicts regarding sexual identity or sexual orientation, and shyness or reservations about sex.

At the other extreme, remember the last time you were too exhausted for sex and double or triple the fatigue you experienced. This may give you some indication of how your bipolar partner feels when her medication dulls her out. Engaging sexually in this frame of mind may seem to be a daunting task rather than an enjoyable and nurturing activity.

Keep in mind that depression plays havoc on a person's sex life. Think about the last time you felt sad. If you sought comfort through sex, you were probably disappointed as it most likely failed to lift your mood. Perhaps you even wanted to be alone. Many factors, unrelated to medication, may influence your bipolar partner's moods and make him unresponsive to sex.

Case Study: Marsha and Peter

Diminished libido may also be the outcome for a partner who experiences frequent disappointment, rejection, or, worse, ridicule and shaming based on what her partner says or does. When extreme, such hurt may even lead to the avoidance of touch as an expression of intimacy. This was Marsha's experience with her husband, Peter, whom she described as becoming increasingly critical of her in the recent years of their marriage.

Marsha says, "We were together for several years before getting married. I knew he had bipolar disorder. I also knew he could be somewhat irritable and, yes, there were times when he seemed quick to criticize or devalue me. But, for the most part, we enjoyed a wonderful relationship. Our sexual life was great and we were quite affectionate.

"As time passed, however, he seemed to become increasingly mean and critical. He would put me down for the way I cooked a dinner, for my selection of clothing — even for my choice of friends. I attributed his behavior to the bipolar illness and, over time, I became uncomfortable saying anything to him since I was afraid of making him even more upset. Gradually, I found myself lacking any desire to be physically intimate with him. I must admit that, in hindsight, my lack of desire was the impetus for his further withdrawal and increased irritability. The more difficult he became to live with, the less interested I was in touching him, until I shunned any form of physical contact with the man whom I had once loved so deeply."

Marsha sought counseling because she truly wanted to work on the marriage, but she was too timid to acknowledge to Peter how strongly she had been impacted by his behavior. Marsha later said, "I blamed Peter's illness for his behavior. I've never been able to assertively express my feelings, especially anger. Actually, I was feeling hurt but thought it my duty to try harder to satisfy him."

Together, Marsha and Peter were playing out their feelings without openly addressing them. In time, his criticism led to her withdrawal and, ultimately, to his abandonment, which precipitated a buildup of isolation. This pattern intensified as Peter began to seek physical intimacy outside of his marriage. While this dance can occur in any relationship, Peter's bipolar illness was in large part responsible for his unfaithfulness.

When Marsha discovered Peter's infidelity, she was quick to minimize her pain and anger because of her ongoing struggle with self-worth. Her discomfort regarding sex — even touching — stemmed from an escalating sense of hurt and shame, and the feeling of inadequacy about not measuring up to Peter's expectations. Although unaware of her subliminal feelings, Marsha had become disgusted with Peter. Through therapy, Marsha gradually regained a sense of trust and was able to express her feelings for Peter. As an outgrowth of her self-awareness and improved self-confidence, Marsha committed herself to work on salvaging the marriage. As a contingency for staying together, with which Peter agreed to comply, Marsha demanded that he consent to couples counseling and individual therapy to work out his degrading behavior toward her.

When Sex Seems Out of Control

Many people immediately identify fidelity as a major component in their relationship. While some partners may engage in physical intimacy outside of their committed relationships, the bipolar partner is more vulnerable to having an affair than his nonbipolar counterpart. Sexual acting out is a common symptom of mania and, in the throes of mania, sexually compulsive behavior can be about the need to prove one's grandiosity. Sex is a way of feeling worshipped or admired. A word of caution: remember that your partner may seek intimacy with a con artist or someone who is physically violent, has a sexually transmitted disease, or does not practice safe sex. Besides the normal hurt and anger that is the aftermath of infidelity, your bipolar partner may be endangering both of your lives.

The signs of infidelity may include your partner working late hours at the office, mysterious weekend "business" or "fishing" trips, sudden gifts of guilt, and so on. If the mania is severe, perhaps no

143

explanation will be offered and your partner will instead make it seem like you are the one who is nosey and critical. Since mania triggers paranoia and feelings of persecution, your partner may even try to argue that you drove him to it or that you are going to use this against him in a divorce and take him for every penny he is worth. He may even accuse **you** of being unfaithful.

You may feel uncomfortable distrusting your partner and subsequently ignore the evidence that he may be acting out sexually. This may increase your distrust still further and lead you to feel even more isolated and resentful. Your concerns need to be expressed, and the best approach is one that emphasizes your hurt and genuine caring in addition to the anger you understandably may experience.

It's also possible that you will become the target of your partner's heightened sexual interest. This may be challenging at a time when your trust is diminished or when your partner is behaving in ways that make you want to withdraw. Being cajoled, accused, or name-called into another round of sex may signal the onslaught of sexual mania. At the same time, it may also be an opportune time to openly discuss how to spice up your sex life. An honest discussion can enhance the trust you experience with each other.

If explicit requests for sex reach a point that they violate your comfort zone, the problem may be as simple as a lack of sleep. You also may not be in the mood for sex, or your partner may demand things you don't want to do. Your personal needs must also be respected, and under no circumstances should you feel you must comply with any sex act that might be unsafe. Depending on the specifics of your partner's bipolar symptoms, you may even fear exposing yourself to a sexually transmitted disease — especially if you know that he has been sexually active with other people. If you and your partner have already had sex after you discover he has had a sexual liaison with another person, both of you may want to be tested for HIV.

If your partner is in the throes of a severe manic episode, call her doctor or take her to the hospital. If your partner suffers from hypomania (mild mania) and little can be done medically to treat her, try to initiate a new strategy of open communication about such matters. You might say, "I'm tired," or "I'd rather not do that," and hope that your needs will be respected as in any other relationship. Failing this, you might try to suggest that both of you get some sleep or perhaps substitute a massage for sex so your partner still feels connected and loved. You might also try to distract her with interesting conversation, a book, a computer game, or even some comfort food — whatever it is that you feel she might enjoy.

If your partner engages in sexually risky behavior, you may feel that you have no choice but to end the relationship, or you may accept the risk and stay committed. If you choose the latter, seek couples counseling and make it clear to your partner that this kind of behavior will not be tolerated again.

Since I am the one with bipolar, it is sometimes challenging for me to feel like I'm being a good parent. I don't want my kids to see me crying or to feel like they are the cause of me being in a bad mood. I try my best to hide my mood swings from my kids, and my spouse does a good job of recognizing when I need a break. I don't always stand up and say I need a break when I actually do need a break to collect my thoughts and emotions, and that is something I need to improve. Your children pick up on the energy you put forth, so many times my kids will misbehave when I am in a bad mood. Then everything escalates, and not in a good way. My spouse sometimes makes me feel like I can't handle being a parent, which is one of my pet peeves. I think he believes that if he wasn't around, the children wouldn't be taken care of since I cannot control my moods. Even though I know deep down that I am a good parent, he makes me feel inadequate. When I am in a bad mood, it is best to let him take the lead with the kids until I have a chance to feel better. Communicating when you need to take a break from the kids is a good way to avoid any disagreements. It should be a tag team effort so that the kids get the best of both parents as much as possible.

Each day brings its share of daily tasks and responsibilities. The central theme for all of these is teamwork. Even if one person has bipolar, acting as a team can greatly benefit both spouses. It removes the pressure from one person if they are having a bad day, without allowing resentment to build. If one person needs to take a break from their responsibilities, it is always nice for that person to show appreciation to the other at a later time. After all, without that other person, every task would be their sole responsibility, and life would be much more difficult.

Chapter 12: Finding Help In Healthy Living

While your brain might not be at it's healthiest you can help it by making sure that the rest of your body is. A healthy lifestyle is an important management technique. What you eat and how much you sleep can greatly affect how well your symptoms affect you. Many people who don't stick to a schedule also don't stick to healthy habits. With an unhealthy lifestyle, you can also foster weight gain, and even trigger depression, making the symptoms worse. Not sticking to your routine is bad, but sticking to a bad one is worse, and you'll only make the problem worse over time. It's such a small change there's really no excuse not to make your routine a healthy one.

Nutrition

What you eat can really affect your mood, but despite the fact that chocolate is a proven anti-depressant it doesn't mean you should live on it. Your food is actually fuel for your body and it contains a host of different vitamins and nutrients. These help in the production of the very chemicals your brain produces and is affected by. Eat too little of the ones it needs and your body physically cannot produce the chemicals it needs for your brain to feel better. For some people eating is a tool to feel better, but this can foster obesity and an unhealthy dependence on food.

Most people reach for rich, sugary or fatty foods when they feel down because they have a natural boosting effect. The problem is these are high in calories and aren't high in nutritional value. Sugar is the biggest culprit. It's been proven to be as addictive as many drugs since it releases both opioids and dopamine to make you feel "good". It fosters addictive behavior with withdrawals and cravings but it also creates anxiety and the hypoglycemia of a sugar crash. Eating products with sugar in actually creates a cycle similar to that of bipolar and should be avoided as much as possible.

Rather than filling up on sugary or refined foods look for those that are nutrient dense. This includes a variety of whole foods, fruits, and vegetables. You'll want to avoid alcohol as well because this is essentially liquid sugar, as well as juices and soda. Artificial sweeteners are just as bad as sugar though with fewer calories and should also be avoided since they cause the same dependency and instability.

Processed and sugary foods can also lead to inflammation, this can physically affect the brain and how it works, causing more stress on the body. Inflammation is also linked to poor immune response and weight gain so you want to avoid it if possible.

Nutrient Therapy

A rather interesting alternative therapy that has come about from our body's own process of cravings. Scientists have begun to analyze exactly what it is that has us reaching for the fridge and how the components affect the brain. In fact, science is strongly supporting that daily vitamin supplements and certain amino acids can positively reduce symptoms as they are converted into the chemicals the brain needs. Unlike traditional medications, there are no side effects and they are much cheaper.

The most popular supplement for bipolar sufferers is an Omega-3 Fatty Acid. This is often found as fish oil. A poor ability to process these acids has been diagnosed in patients and mimics the inhibition of neurotransmitter pathways which are a characteristic of bipolar disease. Just 2g per day of these added supplements have been shown to reduce depressive episodes by 50%.

Vitamin C and Folic acid have also been shown to be important for bipolar sufferers. Those with the disease often have raised homocysteine levels, often the response by the body to low folate and inadequate vitamin C intake. Patients that have functional deterioration consistently show a higher level of homocysteine in their plasma.

Sleep

While fostering a suitable sleep routine is part of managing your symptoms this can be one of the hardest things to follow for sufferers. There are plenty of times when having bipolar disorder actually stops you from having a decent sleep schedule. Consistent sleep patterns are almost as important as a stable routine. Too little or too much sleep are both dangerous and can cause a swing.

Healthy sleep habits include setting a bed and wake up time that is continuous each day, even on weekends. Allowing yourself to "Sleep in" because you feel like it is often a crack for letting depressive habits take hold. A common symptom of depression is sleeping too much, so if you're going to bed at a reasonable time then you don't need to worry about sleeping in. Napping similarly is not helpful because it interrupts your need for sleep at night and can also cause weight gain. By napping, you're burning fewer calories and having less opportunity to take part in activities that could improve your symptoms instead.

Caffeine is a big problem for most people, not just bipolar sufferers. Avoid caffeine after lunch as this can cause you to stay up unnecessarily late. Laptop, TV, and phone screens are also similarly disruptive and should be avoided in the evening. While you should already be avoiding sugar it can have the same effect. Healthy sleep habits also mean not eating or drinking immediately before bed as you'll likely need to get up for the bathroom or because of indigestion. Try not to eat anything for an hour before bed.

Treatments

Take multivitamins and fish oil supplements as an alternative form of nutrient therapy. Deficiencies and low intake of the elements needed for your body to produce the right chemicals may contribute to greater symptoms. Leading a healthy lifestyle that includes plenty of sleep can also help to balance your regime and make you more stable.

Chapter 13: Stories Of Coping And Courage

These are some of the stories that members of my support group have made the decision to share with you so that you can enhance your understanding of what feelings one has when they are diagnosed with a mood disorder. This also helps you to determine what treatment options are available, the manner in which you can deal with matters that surround your relationships, career and social life. This also includes what has worked for them while coping with their mental illnesses. The main theme in this chapter is to ensure that you and I fight social stigma that has been at the forefront of preventing people from seeking help. The importance of this is coming to the realization that there is hope in recovery irrespective of what circumstances stand in the way.

In spite of the fact that each story, in this case, is different and unique in their own way, the truth is that they all resonate around the same themes. These themes are;

Hope- they all have a strong belief that they will soon get well.

Support- they all have sought help from a wide range of sources. These sources include, but is not limited to, therapists, doctors, families, friends, support groups among others.

Determination- they continue seeking the best treatment they can get. This is evident through the kind of dedication they have to improve their health conditions.

Commitment- they all have demonstrated commitment by sticking to their treatment plans despite the challenges that they have faced and the relapses associated with some medications.

Before we can delve into what each bipolar disorder patient has to say about their journey, it is important to note that depression and mania in bipolar patients do not translate into weakness and being flawed. Rather, we have to understand that this illness affects over 20 million people across the globe. With the correct form of treatment, it is possible to manage the symptoms associated with the disorder without necessarily interfering with your life. When you seek treatment for your mental illness, it does not mean that you have failed in any way. It only means that you are strong enough and have the self-courage and sense of feeling better.

The stories here are of different patients at different stages of their illnesses and wellness. The one thing to remember is that it often takes different time frames before a correct diagnosis is made or even before right treatment is found for you. Some have had to try a wide range of methods or even be patient until their treatment is effective. Despite the fact that this is very challenging, the most important thing is holding on to faith and be optimistic that things will work out. If you are suffering from the same condition as the rest of us, do not give up. The key to your recovery is keeping the right mindset, be persistent in your search for the right treatment and the right support from the people around you.

Mercy

Mercy is a young lady who has struggled with bipolar disorder for a very long time without knowing it. What stands out for her is the fact that she has struggled with depression since her early childhood. This is highlighted by the fact that she did not want to take medication. She noted, that despite the fact that her doctors prescribed medications, she just wouldn't take them. However, along the journey, she had to accept her condition and begin taking medications for the sake of her daughter. At the very beginning, antidepressants seemed promising in managing her depression until the time when she became manic and had to be hospitalized. After many years of suffering, she finally received the correct diagnosis of bipolar disorder and received the treatment she needed.

What worked? - The correct diagnosis that caused the doctor to prescribe mood stabilizers and antipsychotics. Additionally, her medication was even made effective by simply getting support from her daughter, family, friends and her church. Through this, she and her daughter have learned so much about bipolar disorders. Though she might have drifted a little due to stress, she continues to work closely with her doctors to make her treatment plan effective.

Matthew, 19 years

Matthew has been in and out of the hospital for a very long time. Just a few months ago, he had a major manic episode while in college. At the time, he was using drugs with his friends before he felt a sudden impulse came over him. This was not the effects of the drugs they had been using because the effect had already worn out. As he recalls, the day after, he felt as though he was on top of the world and owned everything in the universe. He felt as though spending time sleeping was a great waste of time and so he stayed up all night reading and writing poems, a gift he did not know he had. He then spent the following day shopping around for luxurious items such as clothes, shoes, food and treating friends to lunch and dinner. Coming home, Matthew's mother noticed that he was manic because his sister is also bipolar. This is when he was taken to the hospital.

What has worked? - Well, according to Matthew, things are always in place as long as he is on medication. At first, he was afraid that the medication would change his personality and this is the reason why he was still living in denial about him having a mental illness. Matthew was hospitalized a number of times for discontinuing his medications, he hated the hospital but he had to keep taking his meds in order to get well. Additionally, whenever he had manic episodes, he would say stuff he could not take back, and this he said, cost him two girlfriends and thus, he resorted to taking medications.

With the help of family, doctors and a sister who is bipolar too, Matthew has managed well. Additionally, he joined a foundation for bipolar patients which has been very beneficial in helping him cope through the acceptance phase. Now, he has a support treatment team that helps him to stay away from drugs and thus stabilizing his medication and moods.

Yolanda, age 44

Yolanda was adopted from an orphanage in Japan when she was a year and a half old. She was so much neglected in the orphanage and because of this, she was suffering from stunted growth and had challenges walking. According to her, the trauma of her childhood was the main contributing factor to her depression. She narrates a story of when she was a child and wrote in her journals that she died of malaria. The main reason for this is her hopelessness that made her believe she was not going to last beyond a certain age. After the birth of her second child, she fell into the worst depression ever! Whenever her baby cried in the crib, she would be in agony and anguish. She would remember her childhood as an orphan. She would get upset and became harmful to herself. Five years later, she became suicidal and was hospitalized. It was this time that she received a correct diagnosis for bipolar disorder.

What has worked?   -
She says that she has to adhere to medications. Her close working relationship with her doctor has been very beneficial in making relevant adjustments

in her medications to reduce the side effects while ensuring that depression is controlled. Her regular contact with friends has been very instrumental in supporting her through treatment and mood stability. She now enjoys motherhood and enjoys engaging in recreational activities such as; playing the piano and guitar for relaxation. When she is depressed, she is reminded by her support team of her positive traits and the love of her children.

Mark, age 67

He was first diagnosed with bipolar disorder in 1980. However, he threw away all his medications because he had not come to terms with the fact that he was indeed bipolar. While on a business trip, he had a manic episode. He thought that he could develop wings and fly. When he got home, his family wanted him hospitalized. He stayed in the hospital for three days and spent that time praying. Mark hoped that once he was released from the hospital, he would never have to suffer from the illness anymore. This is when he joined DBSA group in California where they worked together with his wife to get more groups started to support people like him.

What has worked? – According to Mark, once he accepted that he was having a problem, it served as the key to getting the help that he needed. He says that he surrounded himself with people who had bipolar disorder and sharing their experiences has extremely helped in his recovery process. By joining a support group he has changed his life. He continues to inspire people today by motivating and encouraging them that they can get better. He is determined to employ any method he can to tell his story to the world so that they can get the healing they need whether people agree with it or not.

Jane, age 52

As a freshman in college several years ago, Jane first experienced depressive episodes that adversely affected her performance in school and this caused her to leave school for a year. After her graduation, she had another severe episode of depression that made her suicidal. She would drive around town looking for somewhere she could purchase a gun from. This is the point where she realized that she needed help and she sought for it. Jane was diagnosed with depression and she was put on psychotherapy. However, even so, she was not getting proper treatment because all the treatment was aiming at was to fix her sexual orientation. One night, she did not have sleep and kept thinking of how to restructure certain psychiatric theories and sharing this with her doctor, she was diagnosed with bipolar disorder.

What has worked? – The fact that she herself is a trained professional psychiatrist. Therefore, she knows that mood disorder does not last forever and thus playing a key role in helping her cope with her mental illness. She is also well aware of the many drugs on the market that come up each day aiming to improve her condition. This is the thing which drives her to try them and hang on to the hope that she can get better. Her strong spiritual belief in God has helped her so much in asking God to grant her serenity to accept the things that she cannot change. Her partner also offers incredible support to make her constantly aware that she is not a failure.

Ricardo, age 60

It was 1979 that Ric experienced the worst depressive episodes of his life. Unfortunately, in 1980, he had another severe manic episode. While in New York, he spent a long period of time seeking the right treatment but it never came through. This is when he and the wife decided that the best thing to do was to learn from people who were suffering from the same disease and how they were coping with their conditions. They started a group in 1981 which has since grown into a whole institution that supports bipolar patients.

What has worked? – He says that one of the things he is grateful about is the fact that he has been free from bipolar episodes for over 20 years. This, he says is due to excellent treatment by his psychopharmacologist, a supportive wife, dedicated work with a psychologist and his work for the community of people living with bipolar disorder. He admits that the greatest challenge is that of self-stigma, guilt and being a hypochondriac. However, working closely with support teams has enabled him to win back his confidence and appreciate his leadership skills.

Jennifer, age 45

Over the years, it is really sad to hear that Jennifer grew up to have tantrums and tendency to cry for no reason whatsoever. She says that she would sometimes break every glass in her house. The main reason for this is that she would anger over small things and destroy everything, then go to bed and feel at peace. She then decided to find treatment from a doctor. However, her family discouraged her telling her that medication was bad, the doctors around were unqualified, and that only if she had faith, she would get well. She heeded to their advice and tried to take control of her episodes by herself. However, as years went by, her situation was getting worse and she decided to get help. She tried several doctors and finally got one who gave her the right prescription.

What has worked? – According to her, the support she gets from her husband is priceless. This is because he helps her stay up to date with information that revolves around bipolar disorder. He also ensures that she never stops her medication and whenever she is not well, he would be the one that supports her and takes care of the home and do the house chores. They often talk about their feelings freely so that they do not end up resenting each other. Working with her doctor is another contributing factor to her getting better. With her doctor, she is able to keep a diary that helps her keep track of her moods which helps in tracking her progress.

Chapter 14: Lifestyle Changes

As mentioned earlier, lifestyle change is necessary in managing symptoms of bipolar disorder. The following lifestyle tips make living with bipolar disorder bearable:

Run Away From Stress

Stress is the major trigger of both manic and depressive episodes. So, if you want to minimize or avoid these episodes, you have to keep stress at bay. Here are some of the things that you can do to reduce stress and promote relaxation:

Keep your personal space and work space organized and clutter free. If you have a bipolar disorder, you have a lot of mental clutter in your mind. So, to avoid racy thoughts, it would help to keep your work and personal space neat and orderly. Also, make sure to label all your drawers. This way, it will be easier for you to find stuff. Make it a habit to sweep your floor at least once a week and then make sure that your things are well organized. It's also best to vacuum and remove all the dust at least twice a week.

Listen to upbeat or soothing music. As mentioned earlier, music has a relaxing effect so whenever you're feeling depressed, put on your headset and play uplifting music. You can also play dance songs and inspirational music. When you're restless, you can play slow and relaxing music. This will help calm and relax your nerves. When you're feeling the work pressure, take a break and play some relaxing music.

List down all your worries and worry about one thing at a time. This will help you feel more relaxed.

Write a journal or start a blog. Writing about your experiences, challenges, and worries will help manage your moods.

Stay away from the toxic people in your life. These are the people who criticize you. Toxic people are those who will try to bring you down and who will do anything to make you feel unhappy. These people will also try to take advantage of you so stay away from them.

Learn to relax. Anxiety and stress can aggravate the mood symptoms of people with bipolar disorder, so it is important to make an effort to relax. After work, sit down and watch your favorite TV show. You can also go out of your friends or perhaps go to the spa and get a massage.

Don't take life and yourself too seriously. To help manage your symptoms. You have to refrain from taking life too seriously.

Learn to crack some jokes at work. You can also watch funny TV shows and movies. You also watch some funny clips on YouTube, too.

Recognize at least one good thing that happened today. Every day, take time to think about at least one good thing that happened during the day. This exercise will realize that your day is not that bad and your life is also not that bad.

Hug the people that you love. Hugging the people that you love is extremely therapeutic. You can hug your pets, too.

Take a break. When everything seems too overwhelming, step back and take a break. This will help clear your mind and avoid the occurrence of either manic or depressive episode.

Exercise

Exercise can help stabilize your mood. It helps control and balance the neurotransmitters in your brain. In fact, it promotes the production of serotonin, endorphins, and other hormones and neurotransmitters that have a mood stabilizing effect. Plus, exercising could help you manage your weight and keep your body fit and healthy. You can do a lot of exercises, including:

Running

Running is a fantastic exercise. It improves your endurance and it also helps you lose weight. Running is also a great way to release those endorphins and serotonin. To manage your bipolar disorder, you can run or jog for at least 30 minutes a day. But, you have to be careful with this exercise, especially if you are having a manic episode. Limit your physical activity to, at most, 2 hours per day. Excessive exercise or physical activity is a symptom of mania so be careful.

Cycling

You can bike around your neighborhood every morning, too. This exercise will increase your heart rate. This will help you burn calories and help manage your symptoms, too.

Yoga

Yoga is an amazing exercise that has many mental health benefits. It improves your cognitive function and it helps manage your mood, too. It helps bipolar patients get and stay in touch with their thoughts and body. This helps the patients become more aware of their mood swings.

Indeed, yoga helps reduce anxiety, depression, neurotic symptoms, and anger. Here are some of the yoga poses that help ease the symptoms of bipolar disorder:

1. Utthita Marichyasana or Standing Sage Marichi Pose

This pose stimulates the part of your body called the cerebellum. This helps you control your emotions.

Photo Source: sacdt.com

2. Hand to Leg Pose or Padahastasana

This pose improves the blood flow to your brain. So, it helps improve cognitive function and it helps you manage your moods, too.

Photo Source: doctorcancer.org

3. Bhumi Pada Mastakasana or "Feet, Hand, and Head on Earth" Pose

This is a deep forward bend exercise. This pose also improve the blood flow to the brain. This pose is a bit challenging, so you

have to do this under the supervision of a
yoga teacher.

Photo Source: youtube.com

Yoga can help manage your moods. It can
also make your life better in many other
ways. It helps you stay grounded. It helps
you focus on the present moment. It also
helps decrease hallucinations, delusions,
and other episodes.

Aside from yoga, running, and biking, you
can also try a lot of other exercises. You

can try dancing and swimming. But, remember to exercise moderately.

Create A Strong Support Group

When you're suffering from bipolar disorder, it is important to create a strong support group. Remember that medications and psychotherapy can only do so much. So, you have to seek help from the people around you. You have to confide in people who you trust. Tell them your struggles and your fears. Also, ask for understanding from people around you. Dealing with bipolar disorder is not easy, but it can be bearable, especially if you surround yourself with loving and understanding people.

Join bipolar support groups. You can also join civic clubs. These clubs will keep you entertained during depressive episodes and grounded during manic episodes.

Make it a habit to talk to someone you care about at least once a day. Go out as much as you can and avoid social isolation.

Get Enough Sleep

Sleep is important for people with bipolar disorder. So, to manage your moods, you have to get at least eight hours of sleep daily. It is also important to establish a fixed sleeping schedule. This means that you have to sleep and wake up at the same time daily.

Don't Put A Lot of Tasks on Your Plate

When you have a manic episode, you'll feel like you can do anything so it is best to avoid putting a lot of tasks your plate. This will help prevent stress and anxiety.

Take Care of Your Self

People with bipolar depression often stay at home for weeks. They do not eat well and they don't even take a bath. So, to manage your bipolar symptoms, you have to take care of yourself. You must practice good hygiene and make sure to take a bath every day. Also, make sure to see your friends often because this will give you a strong sense of belongingness. Try to do something that you truly enjoy every day. You can write or you can paint. Find healthy ways to express yourself and your feelings.

Practice Gratitude

When you're experiencing bipolar depression, you'll feel like you are the unluckiest person in the world. You'll feel like you are carrying all of the problems in life. When this happens, try to look at the bright side and start counting your blessings.

Be thankful that you are alive. Living with bipolar disorder is not easy, but there are still a lot of things to be thankful about.

Be grateful for the people around you, especially those who love and support you.

Be grateful for all the material things that you have right now. If you have a roof over your head, a car, and a job, you are one lucky person so stay grateful.

Even when you're struggling with bipolar disorder, you are still more blessed than you think. So, be grateful.

Stay in Touch With Reality

As discussed earlier in this book, mindfulness is important because it keeps people in touch with reality. Mindfulness is most important for people who suffer from bipolar disorder.

So, if you have bipolar disorder, you have to practice mindfulness in everything that you do.

While you are typing, pay attention to how your fingers hit the each key on the keyboard.

Eat like a food critic. Pay attention to the appearance of the food. Also, take time to notice the different flavors of your food.

Watch your thoughts. Pay attention to your thoughts. What are your self-defeating thoughts? What are your delusions of grandeur? Do you think that you do not deserve love and happiness? Do you think that you are meant to save the world? Well, here are some affirmations that will help keep you grounded:

I deserve love.

I am worthy.

I am a valuable person.

I am worthy and valuable, but I don't believe that I am special

I think that I am pretty much like other people.

I don't have special powers. I am intelligent, but my intelligence is not some kind of a superpower.

I take responsibility for my actions.

I have to avoid reckless behavior.

I will think things through before I make a decision.

To control both your manic and depressive symptoms, you have to keep yourself grounded.

Healthy Diet

Healthy diet is essential for people with bipolar disorder. We will discuss this in detail in the next chapter.

Clean Living

To effectively manage your bipolar symptoms, you have to avoid alcohol and illegal drugs. All your efforts will be thrown out of the window if you still drink alcohol and take illegal drugs. You must take responsibility for yourself and avoid the things that may trigger your mood problems.

Take Note of Your Moods

It is absolutely necessary to take note of your moods. This will help you manage your symptoms more effectively. Each day, write down how you feel in a journal. Also pay attention to your suicidal thoughts.

Whenever you have thoughts of death or suicide, you have to ask for help right away.

The fight against bipolar disorder is not an easy one. But, it can be done. So, you have to be proactive and take the necessary steps to change your lifestyle. Forming new healthy habits can save your sanity and even your life.

Conclusion

Bipolar disorder or manic depressive disorder is a very serious mental and psychological ailment which requires prolonged medical treatment. Sometimes patients need to take a maintenance dosage of medication almost throughout their lives. So, the best thing is to accept the illness and take the necessary action. However, in society, there are a lot of preconceived notions about the disease. Therefore, people first refuse to accept the diagnosis. That is a wrong thing to do. People generally start believing only after the first major manic episode. This should be avoided. One has to trust his doctor and believe what he or she says, so that appropriate measures can be initiated, before things get out of hand.

Society has an important role to play in the recovery and rehabilitation of bipolar disorder victims. People should accept this disease like something similar to blood pressure or diabetes.As this disease has a very high possibility of relapse, the caregivers of the affected person should be empathetic towards the subjects. Medicines should never be stopped without the doctor's advice. Moods of the concerned person must be self monitored at all times. This helps to recognize crisis situations and emergencies instantly. Proper relaxation techniques as advised by the therapist should be followed so as to not heat up the brain too much. The brain circuits, thereby, will not go haywire and cause any emotional roller-coasters.

www.ingramcontent.com/pod-product-compliance
Lightning Source LLC
Chambersburg PA
CBHW060322030426
42336CB00011B/1162